D0093221

> **There is properly no history,**
> **only biography.**
> **— *Ralph Waldo Emerson***

★ ★ ★ ★ ★ ★ ★ ★ ★ ★ ★ ★ ★ ★ ★ ★

he Making of America series traces the constitutional history of the United States through overlapping biographies of American men and women. The debates that raged when our nation was founded have been argued ever since: *How should the Constitution be interpreted? What is the meaning, and where are the limits, of personal liberty? What is the proper role of the federal government? Who should be included in "we the people"?* Each biography in the series tells the story of an American leader who helped shape the United States of today.

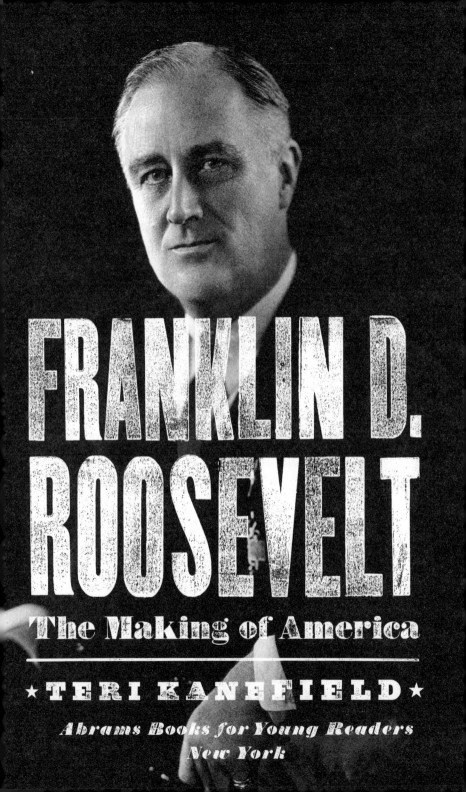

FRANKLIN D. ROOSEVELT

The Making of America

★ TERI KANEFIELD ★

Abrams Books for Young Readers
New York

✷ ✷ ✷ ✷ ✷ ✷ ✷ ✷

Title page: FDR in 1933.

All images used in this book are public domain (National Archives and Library of Congress) with the following exceptions: Pages 9, 11, 15, 21, 29, 36, 40, 49, 54, 70, 108, 114, 132, 137, 156, 164, 184, 209, courtesy of the Franklin Delano Roosevelt Library. Page 143, courtesy of Granger Historical Picture Archive. Page 182, courtesy of AP Images.

Cataloging-in-Publication Data has been applied for and may be obtained from the Library of Congress.

ISBN 978-1-4197-3402-1

Text copyright © 2019 Teri Kanefield
Edited by Howard W. Reeves
Book design by Sara Corbett

Printed and bound in U.S.A.
10 9 8 7 6 5 4 3 2 1

Abrams Books for Young Readers are available at special discounts when purchased in quantity for premiums and promotions as well as fundraising or educational use. Special editions can also be created to specification. For details, contact specialsales@abramsbooks.com or the address below.

ABRAMS The Art of Books
195 Broadway, New York, NY 10007
abramsbooks.com

CONTENTS

FDR in 1933

America Under Attack

n the morning of Sunday, December 7, 1941, at about 8:30, Franklin Delano Roosevelt, President of the United States, was in his private suite on the second floor of the White House, reading his newspapers as he waited for his valet to help him into his wheelchair. For twenty years—since an illness at the age of thirty-nine—he'd been paralyzed from the waist down.

As he waited, he flipped through the *New York Times*, the *Herald Tribune*, two Washington, D.C., papers, and even the *Chicago Herald*, a paper he despised. For the past two years, the newspapers had been blaring ominous news: German tanks rolled into Poland! Nazi Germany conquered Belgium, Holland, and Luxembourg! The Nazis marched into Paris! German bombs were blitzing England! German tanks thundered into Moscow! Fascist Italy conquered Albania! Japan invaded Manchuria, China, and the oil production zones of Borneo and Central Java!

Now Japan and the United States were on the brink of war. The day before had brought alarming news when United States intelligence officers intercepted a fourteen-part message Japan had sent to its Western diplomat. At 3:00 p.m. the message had been sent to Washington, D.C., where intelligence officers set to work deciphering the code. Just before Roosevelt had gone to bed the night before, an officer had come to tell him that the first thirteen parts had been deciphered. They appeared to be a set of resolutions to the United States government detailing why negotiations had broken down.

That morning—as Roosevelt was reading his newspapers—intelligence officers across town were already at work, deciphering the final part. Within a few hours, they broke the code and learned that Japan planned to cut off diplomatic relations with the West at 1:00 p.m. on the East Coast, which would be 10:00 a.m. on the West Coast, and much earlier throughout the Pacific.

America Under Attack

The officers concluded that Japan was planning a morning attack on the United States. The problem was that nobody knew where. So Secretary of War Henry Stimson ordered warnings telegraphed to United States military bases throughout the Pacific, beginning with the most likely targets of Manila and Panama. He had trouble telegraphing warnings to Hawaii because radio contact was broken. After some delays, he sent the alert by commercial telegraph.

By the time his warning reached headquarters in Pearl Harbor on the Hawaiian island of Oahu, it was too late: Japanese fighter planes were roaring over Pearl Harbor, unleashing a torrent of bombs, catching the sleepy harbor by surprise. The devastating attack obliterated almost the entire American fleet and killed twenty-four hundred sailors, soldiers, and civilians. It was the most catastrophic foreign attack in American history.

★ ★ ★ ★ ★ ★ ★ ★ ★ ★ ★ ★ ★ ★ ★

The USS *Arizona* as it appeared before the attack

E leanor Roosevelt, the president's wife, was entertaining guests for lunch. The president joined the group, but after a short time, he excused himself and wheeled himself from the room. "I was disappointed but not surprised," Eleanor wrote later. "The fact that he carried so many secrets in his head made it necessary for him to watch everything he said, which in itself was exhausting."

Roosevelt and his friend and advisor Harry Hopkins had their lunch in private, in what was then called the Oval Study. After they finished eating, Hopkins stretched out on a couch and they made small talk.

The phone rang. When Roosevelt answered, the White House operator told him the caller was Colonel Frank Knox, secretary of the navy. "Put him on," Roosevelt said.

When Knox came to the line, his voice sounded choked. "Mr. President," he said. "It looks as if the Japanese have attacked Pearl Harbor."

"No!" Roosevelt gasped.

Soon the Oval Study was crowded with cabinet members, aides, and secretaries. Messengers rushed in and out with news. The phone rang almost constantly. All around was panic and hubbub—but Roosevelt had regained his composure. "Deadly

The USS *Arizona* during the attack

calm," was how Eleanor later described him. "His reaction to any great event was always to be calm," she said. "If it was something that was bad, he just became almost like an iceberg and there was never the slightest emotion that was allowed to show." He was so emotionless, in fact, that rumors later circulated that he knew in advance of the attack. Some even claimed he invited the attack as a way to solidify his own power and get America into the war. In fact, Roosevelt, while tightly controlled, was as surprised as everyone else.

He knew the Japanese attack meant that the United States would have to fight a war on two fronts: against Germany in Europe, and Japan in the East. He also knew that America was not prepared. "We haven't got the navy to fight in both the Atlantic and the Pacific," he told Eleanor. "So we will have to build up the navy and the Air Force and that will mean we have to take a good many defeats before we can have a victory."

✱ ✱ ✱ ✱ ✱ ✱ ✱ ✱ ✱ ✱ ✱ ✱ ✱ ✱ ✱

When President Roosevelt had trouble relaxing because he was beset with worries, he had a method for soothing himself. He would close his eyes and imagine himself a boy again at home in Hyde Park, New York, standing with his sled atop the hill that stretched to the wooded bluffs of the Hudson River. He remembered each twist and turn of the hill in such vivid detail that he could visualize himself maneuvering his sled around each obstacle. He imagined reaching the bottom, and then pulling the sled up the hill and zooming down again.

For a few blissful moments, he wasn't the president of the United States about to face a world war—and he wasn't paralyzed from the waist down. He was a carefree boy, home again, sledding on the banks of the Hudson River.

1
Always Bright and Happy

"All that is in me goes back to the Hudson."
— *Franklin Delano Roosevelt*

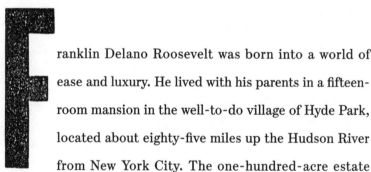

ranklin Delano Roosevelt was born into a world of ease and luxury. He lived with his parents in a fifteen-room mansion in the well-to-do village of Hyde Park, located about eighty-five miles up the Hudson River from New York City. The one-hundred-acre estate featured large stables, a track for his father's racehorses, and a garden house. Franklin had a half-brother, the child of his father's first marriage. His brother was named James for their father, but went by the nickname of Rosy. When Franklin was

Franklin Delano Roosevelt's birthplace in Hyde Park, New York

born, Rosy was twenty-eight years old, and married with a mansion of his own and two small children.

After Franklin was born, the doctors told his mother that she wouldn't be able to have any more children. As a result, she lavished all of her attention on Franklin. Wealthy nineteenth-century mothers generally delegated childcare duties to nurses and nannies, but Sara Delano Roosevelt insisted on caring for her own baby. Franklin's mother was thus the central figure of his early childhood. His father was the energetic companion who taught him to sled before he was two, and to skate, sail, ride a horse, and shoot a hunting rifle as soon as he was old enough. His passions were ships and the sea. "Even as a little mite," Sara said, "he declared himself a sea-faring man."

His father was easygoing. His mother was determined to mold her son into a gentleman, but she did so gently. Young Franklin thus knew nothing of harsh discipline, family quarrels, or anger.

"In thinking back to my earliest days," he said later, "I am impressed by the peacefulness and regularity of things both in respect to places and people." Whether at home in Hyde Park or another of his family residences, his routine was the same: Up at seven, breakfast at eight, lessons until eleven, lunch at noon, more lessons until four, two hours of play, then supper and bed. Franklin's playmates were chosen from among his parents' circle of friends, but Franklin spent most of his time with adults. His tutors, carefully handpicked by his mother, gave him lessons in Latin, French, German, penmanship, history, and arithmetic. During his family's extended stays in Europe, he attended school there and became fluent in both German and French.

One day when Franklin was about eight, Sara noticed that he seemed melancholy. She asked him if was unhappy. He thought for a moment, and then said, "Yes, I am unhappy."

She asked him why. He grew thoughtful. As Sara later told the story: "Then with a curious little gesture that combined entreaty with a suggestion of impatience, he clasped his hands in front of him and exclaimed, 'Oh, for freedom.'" Sara gave the matter some thought, and talked it over with James. The next morning, she told Franklin he could do whatever he pleased that day. He didn't have to obey any of his usual rules and could "roam at will."

For a full day, she paid no attention to him. His tutors had a day off. That evening, he came back to the house muddy, tired, and hungry. "We could only deduce that his adventures had been a little lacking in glamour," Sara later explained, "for the next day, quite of his own accord, he went contentedly back to his routine."

Franklin with his father, James, 1887

Franklin with his mother, Sara, 1887

★　★　★　★　★　★　★　★　★　★　★　★　★　★　★

Franklin's roots went deep in American history. The first Roosevelt to come to America was Claes van Roosevelt, a Dutchman who landed in New Amsterdam (later renamed New York) in 1650. In time, the Roosevelts amassed a fortune in Manhattan real estate and the West Indian sugar trade. Franklin's great-great-grandfather Isaac Roosevelt worked with Alexander Hamilton to persuade the New York legislature to ratify the U.S. Constitution. Among James Roosevelt's close friends was George McClellan, the general who had led Union troops in the Civil War and who challenged Abraham Lincoln for the presidency in 1864.

Like the Roosevelts, Franklin's mother's family, the Delanos, enjoyed the social prestige of being able to trace their ancestry back to America's beginnings. Seven of Sara's ancestors had come to America on the *Mayflower*. Sara's father, Warren Delano, had inherited a small fortune, and amassed a much larger one importing tea and silks from China. Sara was well-spoken and fluent in French and German. In the words of a friend, Sara Delano "had a gift for saying the right thing, and she could say it in several languages."

Sara considered herself an American aristocrat. She believed that her class was superior to other classes, and she believed her race was superior to other races. She also believed that the

Delanos were superior to all other families—including the Roosevelts. She embraced the concept of *noblesse oblige*, which meant
that it was the responsibility of privileged people to act gener-
ously and nobly toward those less fortunate. As a result, she gave
large sums of money to charity. She was poised, regal, beautiful,
and conscious of her position in society.

Franklin's father fell in love with Sara Delano four years after
his first wife died of heart disease. When James Roosevelt proposed marriage, both Sara and her father had reservations. James
was much older. Sara was the same age as his son Rosy. James was
a Democrat. The Delanos were Republicans. Sara's father had a
low opinion of Democrats in general, whom he associated with
rural America and the Confederacy. He was fond of saying, "I will
not say that all Democrats are horse thieves, but it would seem
that all horse thieves are Democrats." But James, who was clearly
in love, was a thoughtful and devoted suitor—and he possessed
an important quality: He was wealthy enough so that the Delanos
didn't have to worry that he was marrying Sara for her fortune.

✳ ✳ ✳ ✳ ✳ ✳ ✳ ✳ ✳ ✳ ✳ ✳ ✳ ✳ ✳

F ranklin was eight years old when his father suffered a
minor heart attack. The robust and energetic James was

13

suddenly sickly and frail. Franklin and Sara, worried that at any moment he could die, plotted ways to protect him from anything that might distress or worry him. Franklin proved to be a tough eight-year-old. When a steel curtain rod fell and slashed his forehead, he bit back his cries to protect his father from distress. When a playmate accidentally hit his tooth with a stick, breaking the tooth and causing Franklin extreme pain, he muffled his cries.

Knowing that he had to be strong because his father was not, Franklin always appeared optimistic and charming, which earned him the approval of the adults around him. Thus by the age of eight he was already developing the personality trait that would later baffle and frustrate his political opponents: his ability to hide his thoughts, feelings, and motives behind a carefully bland face. His maternal grandfather approvingly called him "a very nice child," which, he explained, meant that Franklin was "always bright and happy."

✦   ✦   ✦   ✦   ✦   ✦   ✦   ✦   ✦   ✦   ✦   ✦   ✦   ✦   ✦

Franklin's parents selected the private boarding school he would attend when he turned twelve. Groton School, nestled in the picture-book charm of the Massachusetts countryside, was one of the most exclusive in the country. The school

Franklin at the age
of eleven, 1893

stressed moral growth and public service. The headmaster, Reverend Endicott Peabody, said his goal was to train conscientious men of action, not philosophers and deep thinkers. "I'm not sure I like boys who think too much," said Peabody. "A lot of people think a lot of things we could do without." In his view, "The best thing for a boy is to work hard . . . play hard . . . and then, when the end of the day has come, to be so tired that he wants to go to bed and to sleep."

But Franklin didn't want to go to Groton. He wanted to go to Annapolis and become a naval officer and sea captain. His father talked to him "man to man," and explained that it would be cruel for an only child to be away at sea and so far from his parents. His parents preferred college and a law degree, to prepare him for a gentleman's work. To avoid distressing his father, Franklin accepted his parents' decision.

When Franklin turned twelve and the time came for him to go to Groton, his parents weren't ready yet to part with him. So he stayed with them for another two years, studying with private tutors and accompanying his parents on extended trips to Europe.

In September of his fourteenth year, his parents couldn't postpone his formal education any longer. His trunks were packed, and his parents accompanied him to Massachusetts. As soon as they left him at school, Franklin felt the shock of his new surroundings. His bedroom was a cubicle-sized dorm room. His clothing hung on pegs. The cubicle had a curtain instead of a solid door, so the boys had no real privacy. The morning bell roused the boys at 6:45. Accustomed to warm, leisurely baths, Franklin now found himself herded into an icy shower with two dozen other boys for a quick scrubbing, followed by breakfast, morning chapel, and lessons.

The boys Franklin's age had been at Groton for two years, so friendships had already formed. He thus found himself isolated and "entirely out of things." His new classmates saw none of the strength of character that allowed him to stifle the crushing pain of a broken tooth. They saw a slender, jaunty, well-mannered and well-spoken boy accustomed to the company of adults and not the rough and tumble of boys—exactly the kind of boy likely to be bullied.

Groton School, Groton, Massachusetts

Fortunately Franklin knew instinctively how to respond to bullying. When a group of older students cornered him and jabbed his feet with hockey sticks to make him dance, Franklin hid his fear and threw himself into a wild dance, pirouetting, toe-dancing, and hooting with laughter, as if the incident was great fun. After that the bullies left him alone. So did everyone else. Through it all, he remained "dry-eyed" and "resolute."

He was lonely and homesick, but he didn't let his parents know. To reassure them that he was fine, he lied in letters home. In a letter dated October 1, 1896, he told his parents, "I am getting on very well with the fellows although I do not know them all yet." A few days later, he assured them that "I am very well."

★ ★ ★ ★ ★ ★ ★ ★ ★ ★ ★ ★ ★ ★ ★

Franklin hid more than his fears and feelings. He also hid his sharp intelligence. He blended in as an average student. He did well in his classes, but never excelled.

By the time he was sixteen, he'd grown accustomed to the school, and even made a few friends. He most enjoyed the times when Theodore Roosevelt—his fifth cousin once removed— visited the school and delivered riveting lectures about his public service. "Cousin Theodore" or "Uncle Ted," as Franklin called him, had by that time served as New York police commissioner and speaker in the New York legislature. He was then assistant secretary of the navy—a job that particularly appealed to Franklin, who still longed to be a sea captain.

Both the school master and Sara Delano Roosevelt viewed Teddy Roosevelt as an exemplar of a gentleman who went into politics with the aim of creating a fairer and more just society. Being related to Teddy Roosevelt gave Franklin status at Groton. Franklin was thrilled each time Teddy honored their kinship by inviting Franklin to his family gatherings.

It was at just such a family gathering—a Christmas party in the home of Teddy's sister, Corrine Roosevelt Robinson—that Franklin first took notice of his future wife. Anna Eleanor Roosevelt, who went by the name Eleanor, was daughter of Theodore's younger brother. Theodore always said she was his favorite niece. She was then fourteen, and Franklin was sixteen. They'd known each other all their lives—when they were very young, Franklin had given her rides on his back—but they saw each other rarely.

Like Franklin, Eleanor was born into wealth and privilege. Unlike Franklin, though, her childhood was not a happy one. When she was five, her father, whose foot had been badly injured in an accident, began to drink excessively to dull the pain.

Troubles developed between Eleanor's parents, and he was often gone. In time her parents separated. Her mother was left "desperately lonely and wildly furious." When her father was around, though, he treated Eleanor lovingly, and she idolized him.

Eleanor was a "shy and solemn child" who hadn't inherited her mother's beauty, and who was "lacking the spontaneous joy and mirth of life." Upper-class girls were expected to be cheerful, pretty, and sociable, but Eleanor was none of these things. Somber, less-than-beautiful girls like Eleanor were often pitied by their contemporaries because they had no chance of growing up to be popular, sought-after debutantes. One of Eleanor's earliest memories was her mother mocking her for being so serious.

Eleanor was eight when her mother fell ill with diphtheria. Eleanor and her younger brother, Hall, were sent to live with her maternal grandmother. When news came that her mother had died, Eleanor received the news quietly and solemnly. She was still living with her grandmother a year and a half later when, just before her tenth birthday, her father died of alcoholism. She felt devastated by his death. She was left an orphan, but a wealthy and well-connected one, with a trust fund and a famous last name.

At that particular Christmas party, Eleanor was standing awkwardly by the wall, where she was often found at social events. She disliked parties so much, in fact, she often made up an excuse to leave early. She had a shy habit of looking down at her hands. Franklin approached her and asked her to dance. He later told his mother that "Cousin Eleanor has a very good mind."

✶ ✶ ✶ ✶ ✶ ✶ ✶ ✶ ✶ ✶ ✶ ✶ ✶ ✶ ✶

Franklin's last year at Groton was his best. He made the second football team, although he rarely left the bench

Franklin (*center*) with the Groton football team

during games. Like most of his graduating class, he planned to enroll at Harvard University in Cambridge, Massachusetts.

Over the summer, his father's health worsened. James spent long drowsy hours on the veranda, looking out over the bay. Sara sat with him, tending his needs. Franklin was gone during the days with friends, playing golf, sailing, or attending parties. His parents, idle because of James's illness, had little to do but wait for him to return each evening.

When it was time for Franklin to travel to the Harvard campus, both his parents went with him. Sara furnished the apartment he would share with his roommate Lathrop Brown, a friend from Groton. She ordered drapes, carpets, and furniture. Franklin and Lathrop decorated with Groton pennants and framed football team photographs. Franklin selected his courses. He was drawn to subjects like economics, government, and modern history.

That fall his parents rented a beachside cottage in South Carolina, hoping that a milder winter would be good for James's health. The better climate didn't help. James suffered a heart attack in November. Both Rosy and Franklin joined James and Sara for a brief visit. They all spent an evening in the parlor. James was "very delicate and tired-looking," Sara said, "but it was sweet to be together."

After Franklin returned to school, James grew even weaker. Sara had him moved by train to New York to be closer to his doctors. In early December, he rapidly lost weight and had trouble sleeping. Sara wired Franklin to let him know. Franklin arrived early the next morning. He ran errands and did whatever his father needed, and tried to comfort his exhausted mother.

A few days later, Rosy arrived. Having his two sons with him brightened James's spirits. The evening after Rosy arrived, they all ate dinner together. Later, James was moved to his bed. He couldn't sleep, so his two sons and wife sat with him. Rosy, Sara, and Franklin were still with him when he died in the early hours of December 8, 1900.

Anna
Eleanor
Roosevelt

*"To reach a port, we must set sail—
Sail, not tie at anchor
Sail, not drift."*
— Franklin Delano Roosevelt

ranklin earned mostly C grades his first semester at Harvard, partly because he spent so much time making the social rounds in Boston, handing his calling card to butlers in the city's finest mansions. He was emerging as something of a bon vivant—thoroughly enjoying pleasures like parties, social gatherings, good food, and stimulating conversation. He joined Harvard's Republican Club and attended political events.

His mediocre grades didn't bother him. What bothered him

Franklin at the age of nineteen, in 1900

was that he failed to get elected to Harvard's most exclusive club, the Porcellian Club. His disappointment was particularly bitter because his own father and Cousin Ted, who was now governor of New York, had both been members. Franklin's only real accomplishment his first year was winning a spot on the editorial board of *The Crimson*, Harvard's student newspaper. Mostly he wrote editorials about the need for more school spirit.

During his second semester at Harvard, Cousin Teddy was selected to replace President William McKinley's Vice President Garret Hobart, who had died in office. Cousin Ted was sworn in as vice president of the United States on March 4, 1901. Franklin, who by this time openly idolized his distant cousin, began imitating some of Teddy's mannerisms, including his habit of saying "bully!" and "delighted," pronounced *dee-lighted!*

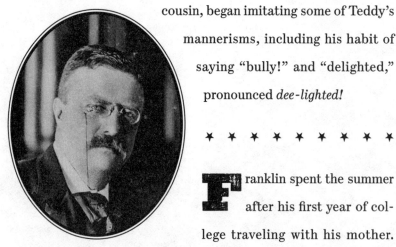

Theodore Roosevelt circa 1901

★ ★ ★ ★ ★ ★ ★ ★

Franklin spent the summer after his first year of college traveling with his mother. He was back at Harvard by

September 6, 1901—the day the nation was shocked by the news that President McKinley had been shot by an assassin, Leon Czolgosz, an anarchist who hated all government and believed it was his duty to kill government leaders. President McKinley died on September 14, 1901. Teddy Roosevelt was hurriedly sworn in as president of the United States in a small private ceremony in Buffalo, New York.

Theodore Roosevelt had such a lively and interesting personality that the newspapers eagerly covered all aspects of his personal and family life. People referred to him as "Teddy." He responded by being quotable. When people complained that his daughter Alice was too wild—she attended too many parties, kept a pet snake, and drove too fast in cars—he said, "I can be President of the United States, or I can control Alice. I cannot possibly do both." A new toy, a stuffed bear, was named after him. The name, Teddy Bear, came about because Teddy refused to shoot a bear during a hunting trip in Mississippi. Cartoons appeared in newspapers all across the country showing the president refusing to shoot the bear. A shop owner in Brooklyn, New York, got the idea to put one of the newly manufactured stuffed bears into his window with a sign that said, "Teddy's Bear."

✦ ✦ ✦ ✦ ✦ ✦ ✦ ✦ ✦ ✦ ✦ ✦ ✦ ✦ ✦

Franklin was tall, slender, good-looking, and rich—but young women were not impressed. Many of them saw nothing of substance behind his jaunty smile. They concluded that he was frivolous and shallow. One of his cousins referred to him as Feather Duster, in a play on his first two initials. She thought Franklin was too chatty, too eager-to-please, and a bit of a mama's boy. His mama's boy image was not helped when his mother, now lonely in her widowhood, took an apartment not far from Harvard so she could be closer to her son. She expected to be just as much a part of his life now as when he was a small boy.

Franklin, like most college students, wanted a life of his own apart from his mother, but he didn't want to hurt her feelings. His habit of secrecy came to his rescue. He told her trivial details about his days, while hiding what was important. He developed a knack for being friendly, warm—and evasive. As a result, Sara had no idea he courted and even hoped to marry two young women during his first two years at Harvard, both of whom turned him down. His penchant for secrecy in fact makes it difficult for biographers to pinpoint his thoughts and feelings during his early years. His mother and Eleanor, in contrast, both left detailed memoirs and autobiographies.

One biographer concluded that "The effort to become his

own man without wounding his mother fostered in him much of the guile and easy charm, love of secrecy and skill at maneuver he brought to the White House." Of course, the analysis could go the other way: Franklin was able to fool his mother because he was naturally charming and deceptive.

One day in the summer of 1902, just before his third year at Harvard, Franklin and Sara were on the New York Central train on their way home to Hyde Park when Franklin spotted Eleanor, who was going to visit her grandmother at her estate farther up the Hudson in Tivoli. Franklin, delighted to see her, sat with her to talk.

After Eleanor and Franklin talked for almost two hours, he took her to say hello to his mother. Sara greeted Eleanor cordially.

Eleanor Roosevelt in 1902

Eleanor had always liked Sara, and now felt struck by her grace and regal beauty. Sara was less impressed with Eleanor. Sara admired girls who were poised, sociable, and outgoing. Like many others in the upper classes of that era, Sara felt disdain for girls who were too serious and intellectual.

Eleanor had recently graduated from the Allenswood Academy for girls in London, where the headmistress, Mademoiselle Marie Souvestre, recognized Eleanor as a gifted student. Souvestre said that Eleanor "influenced others in the right direction. She is full of sympathy for all those who live with her and she shows an intelligent interest in everything she comes in contact with." Souvestre believed Eleanor was destined for a public career, which meant she would not marry. It was understood at the time that a woman could not have both a career and a family. Eleanor, too, assumed she would never marry and that she would dedicate her life to public service—until she fell in love with Franklin, and realized he was in love with her, too.

That fall, Franklin journeyed often from Harvard to New York, where he saw Eleanor at parties, dinners, and social events. He took to inviting her to lunch. He kept a line-a-day diary. Most of his entries were notations of what he did or where he went. He notations were cryptic and rarely gave any indication of his feelings. When he did make an entry that was at all revealing, he wrote in a complicated code for fear that it might fall into Sara's hands. One day, in code, he wrote "E is an Angel." Another day, he wrote in plain language: "Lunch with Aunt K's party." He then switched to code, and wrote, "After lunch I have a never to be forgotten walk to the river with my darling."

Franklin was so guarded that neither Sara nor anyone else among his family or friends had any idea that he and Eleanor were falling in love, even though they were frequently together in the presence of their families. They were together at the New York Horse Show at Madison Square Garden when they sat as Rosy's guest in his private box. Franklin saw her at the White House on New Year's Eve when they both stood with family and watched the president greet thousands of well-wishers. Eleanor was at Franklin's birthday dinner on January 30, 1903, hosted by Rosy and attended by Sara and extended family members.

While Franklin was attending his classes at Harvard, Eleanor was busy with volunteer work. She rode public transportation each day to New York's Lower East Side, where she taught exercise and dance to girls at the Rivington Street Settlement House. She and Franklin didn't see each other much during the spring because Sara wanted to spend so much time with Franklin that he found it hard to get away to New York for weekends. That summer, he and Sara went to Europe. He kept in touch with Eleanor through letters.

Eleanor's younger brother, Hall, enrolled at Groton in the fall of 1903. In October, Franklin invited Eleanor to come to Massachusetts to attend the Harvard-Yale football game. She came for the double purpose of attending the game with Franklin and visiting her brother at Groton. The day after the football game, Franklin accompanied her to Groton. Eleanor and Franklin sat with Hall during the church service in place of his parents.

Later that afternoon, Eleanor and Franklin went for a walk in the nearby woods. It was there that he asked her to marry him. He told her that with her help, one day he would amount to something. "When he told me he loved me," Eleanor later said, "and asked me to marry him, I did not hesitate to say yes, for I knew that I loved him too."

✶ ✶ ✶ ✶ ✶ ✶ ✶ ✶ ✶ ✶ ✶ ✶ ✶ ✶ ✶

Franklin visited his mother to tell her that he'd proposed to Eleanor. Sara received the news with her usual calm. She didn't say much. In her journal she wrote, "Franklin gave me quite a startling announcement." A few weeks later, on December 1, 1903, Franklin took Eleanor to see Sara at the Roosevelt apartment in the Renaissance Hotel. Sara firmly told them that they were too young. She made them promise to keep the engagement secret for a year to test the strength of their commitment.

Both Eleanor and Franklin understood she was jealous and afraid of losing her son. In the coming weeks, both sought to reassure her that she was not losing a son, she was gaining a daughter. "Dearest Mama—I know what pain I must have caused you . . ." Franklin wrote to her, "but now you will have two children to love & who love you." Eleanor also wrote that "I know just how you feel & how hard it must be, but I do want you to learn to love me a little."

Franklin and Eleanor went along with Sara's wishes and kept their engagement secret. Franklin even kept the secret from his roommate and closest friend. He went to New York to see Eleanor as often as he could without his mother finding out.

✷ ✷ ✷ ✷ ✷ ✷ ✷ ✷ ✷ ✷ ✷ ✷ ✷ ✷ ✷

When Franklin graduated from Harvard on June 29, 1903, both Sara and Eleanor were in the audience. Their engagement, though, was still secret. Franklin and Eleanor saw each other a few times over the summer. That fall, he returned to Harvard for the fall semester to take graduate courses so he could prepare for law school. When the semester ended, Sara persuaded Franklin to accompany her on an extended Caribbean cruise, hoping absence would help him forget Eleanor.

The ploy didn't work. When Eleanor and Franklin saw each other again in New York after the long absence, Eleanor recorded in her journal that "Franklin's feelings did not change."

★ ★ ★ ★ ★ ★ ★ ★ ★ ★ ★ ★ ★ ★ ★

In October of 1904—during Franklin's first semester at Columbia Law School—he and Eleanor announced their engagement. Sara might have thought the serious and inward Eleanor unworthy of her son, but other members of New York high society had a different view of the matter: Eleanor was not only sensitive and gifted, she was also the president's favorite niece. Theodore Roosevelt's branch of the family considered the Hyde Park Roosevelts to be the less important and less distinguished branch. Moreover, Franklin seemed to many of his contemporaries to be without substance—a feather duster. The general consensus was that Franklin had made a good match.

The next presidential election was held a month after Franklin and Eleanor announced their engagement. It was the first election in which Franklin was old enough to vote. The voting age for men was then twenty-one; women could not yet vote. Naturally Franklin voted for Cousin Teddy. Theodore Roosevelt, who had been serving as president since McKinley's death, defeated his

Democratic rival, Alton B. Parker, in a landslide victory, winning 56.4 percent of the vote to Parker's 37.6 percent.

✶ ✶ ✶ ✶ ✶ ✶ ✶ ✶ ✶ ✶ ✶ ✶ ✶ ✶ ✶

The newly elected president, Theodore Roosevelt, offered Eleanor a White House wedding, but she preferred to get married in the home of one of her aunts, Maggie Ludlow, who lived on East 76th Street in New York. The wedding took place on March 17, 1905. Two hundred guests attended. Palms and lilacs and roses decorated the house, and an orchestra filled the house with music.

Eleanor was close to six feet tall—almost as tall as her bridegroom. It wasn't the bride, though, who was the center of attention. It was the president, who stood in for Eleanor's deceased father. Theodore enjoyed, and invited, the attention. In fact, Franklin and Eleanor had to leave the receiving line to join the guests, who were thronged around the president. One of Theodore's daughters quipped that when her father attended a wedding, he wanted to be the bride, and when he attended a funeral, he wanted to be the corpse.

The newlyweds moved into a small furnished apartment Sara rented for them on East 65th Street. At the end of Franklin's first

Franklin and Eleanor, 1905

year of law school, they left for a three-month European honeymoon. As distinguished persons, they were invited to eat at the captain's table. In England they were treated almost like visiting royalty because of Eleanor's close kinship to the president. Eleanor felt embarrassed by the fuss. Franklin enjoyed it.

After a few months in Europe, they returned to New York to find that Sara had rented them a grander house on 36th Street. Sara also hired and paid for a cook, a maid, and housekeeper. Franklin and Eleanor both had income from trust funds, but Sara saw to it that they lived a lavish lifestyle far beyond their own means. She even provided them with a summer home and a yacht.

On Christmas, Sara told them she intended to give them, as a Christmas present, a Manhattan house built especially for them. She planned to commission two houses at 47 and 49 East 65th Street, one for her, and one for Franklin and Eleanor. There would be sliding doors between the two houses. Eleanor, who was still young and timid, was not yet challenging the authorities in her life, and didn't question her mother-in-law's constant presence.

Sara had strong opinions on how a house should be decorated. Eleanor deferred to her. Eleanor and Franklin's first child, Anna Eleanor, was born on May 3, 1906. Not surprisingly, Sara also had strong opinions about child raising. Sara took control, hiring and supervising nurses and nannies.

Franklin followed the norms of the era and left the child-rearing to Eleanor and Sara. When he was home, he saw his role in the family as the jovial father who plays with his child. His daughter Anna later described him as "a wonderful playmate who took long walks with you, sailed with you, could out-jump you and do a lot of things."

Franklin didn't take to law school any more than he'd taken to his undergraduate studies. As before, he spent a great deal of his time socializing. Rosy, who lived in New York, helped him meet the most influential New Yorkers. A law degree wasn't necessary to practice law—all he had to do was pass the state exam—so he quit law school and signed up to take the test. He passed on his second try. In 1907, he received his license to practice law in New York.

Sara arranged for Franklin to interview with Edmund L. Baylies, a partner in the illustrious Wall Street law firm of Carter, Ledyard & Milburn. Baylies and Sara belonged to the same yacht club. Not surprisingly, Baylies offered Franklin a job. One of Franklin's first tasks was to record a deed of transfer of some land at the county clerk's office. "I had never been in a county clerk's office," Franklin said. "And there I was, theoretically a full-fledged lawyer."

Franklin was a quick learner and was soon competent in a law library, chasing down references and citations. The firm represented leading corporations: the American Tobacco Company, Standard Oil of New Jersey, and American Express. His colleagues, though, were not particularly impressed with him. "Everyone . . . regarded him as a harmless bust," said one acquaintance years later. "He had a sanguine temperament, almost adolescent in its buoyancy."

On a slow afternoon in the law office, twenty-five-year old Franklin and a few colleagues chatted about their hopes for the future. When it came Franklin's turn, he calmly and matter-of-factly told the group that he intended to become president of the United States. He explained his strategy: He would first get elected to the New York Senate. Then he'd win appointment as assistant secretary of the navy, and after that, he would run for governor of New York. "Anyone who is governor of New York," he explained, "has a good chance to be President, with any luck." The plan happened to be the same route Theodore Roosevelt had followed to the White House. Nobody listening to Franklin laughed. According to one person present, his "engaging frankness" and "sincerity" made his pronouncement seem perfectly natural.

Franklin and Eleanor's second child, James, was born on December 23, 1907. Sara again took control of the nursery and managed the baby's schedule. By this time, though, Eleanor was becoming uncomfortable with Sara in charge of her life. She felt increasingly useless. One day Franklin entered their bedroom to find her sobbing. Astonished, he asked what was wrong. She told him she didn't like living in a house that was not "in any way mine, one that I had done nothing about and which did not represent the way I wanted to live." Franklin couldn't understand her tears. Hadn't she been given the opportunity to comment on the plans? He assured her that she would feel different in a little while, and then left the room until she could calm down.

When Eleanor told the story later she explained that he was

never comfortable talking about emotions or feelings. She also understood that she was just beginning the process of discovering who she was as an individual instead of just "absorbing the personalities of those about me and letting their tastes and interests dominate me."

Franklin and Eleanor with their first two children, Anna and James, 1908

✶ ✶ ✶ ✶ ✶ ✶ ✶ ✶ ✶ ✶ ✶ ✶ ✶ ✶

A third baby, named Franklin Delano Roosevelt, Jr., was born March 18, 1909. The baby's delicate health was a constant worry. All summer, he was sickly and frail. When he was five months old, he developed a cold. Sara hired a special nurse to care for him, but he ate irregularly and steadily lost weight. When a doctor detected a heart murmur, Franklin and Eleanor took the baby to a Manhattan specialist who confirmed that Franklin Jr. had endocarditis, and little hope of surviving.

The baby died on November 1, 1909. Eleanor was devastated. It seemed to her that Franklin, with his usual buoyancy, recovered quickly from the baby's death. Franklin was saddened, but didn't seem deeply affected. Indeed, Franklin didn't say much or show his emotions, but he was more deeply affected than Eleanor understood at the time. He responded to his son's death by joining the board of the New York Milk Committee dedicated to reducing infant mortality in the city. The committee, with storefronts in the poorest and most crowded parts of the city, provided clean milk for babies who needed it and free medical advice for parents who were unable to afford it. Franklin applied himself to the task of saving the lives of babies with energy and dedication.

Entering Politics

> *"There are many ways of going forward,*
> *but only one way of standing still."*
> *— Franklin Delano Roosevelt*

ranklin decided to run for office as a Democrat. Eleanor was expecting another baby when he told her what he intended to do. "I listened to all Franklin's plans with a great deal of interest," she said later. "It never occurred to me that I had any part to play. I felt I must acquiesce in whatever he might decide to do . . . I was having a baby, and for a time at least that was my only mission in life."

Sara, on the other hand, had plenty to say. She was particularly shocked by the Democrat part. Teddy Roosevelt was a Republican. Her own family was Republican, and she firmly believed that Republicanism and respectability went hand in hand. The Republicans, after all, were associated with the educated, urban elites, while the Democrats represented rural America and the former Confederacy. She didn't like the casual way many Democratic politicians dressed, wearing shirts without jackets and clothing associated with laborers.

After Franklin's decision to run as a Democrat became more widely known, Sara told him that a great many of their friends said it was a shame "for so fine a young man to associate with 'dirty' politicians." She agreed with her friends. She had raised him to be a dignified country gentleman, like his father, and she didn't understand why he wanted to associate with working-class politicians whom she viewed as power-grabbers.

Later Franklin explained his choice this way: "My father and grandfather were Democrats and I was born and brought up a Democrat, but in 1904 when I cast my first vote for President, I voted for the Republican candidate, Theodore Roosevelt, because I felt he was a better Democrat than the Democratic candidates."

Franklin's decision to run as a Democrat may have been

shrewder than he let on. The year he entered politics, 1910, the Republican Party was so bitterly divided over labor unions that it seemed to be coming apart at the seams.

✱　✱　✱　✱　✱　✱　✱　✱　✱　✱　✱　✱　✱　✱　✱

F ranklin kicked off his political career by contacting the leaders of the Democratic League of the State of New

By the early twentieth century, railroads and factories had become dangerous places to work. Injuries were common. Injured laborers often lost their jobs and sank into poverty. Industrialists grew wealthy, but continued paying low wages.

The laborers formed unions and demanded better working conditions and better wages. The factory owners resisted, saying they needed flexibility. When laborers looked for government protection, the industrialists railed against the federal government intruding into business. Before the Civil War, Northern industrialists (most of whom were Republicans) wanted a strong federal government to put an end to slavery.

York and telling them he was interested in running for office. The local party leaders in Dutchess County gave Franklin a close look. Some had mixed feelings. Franklin seemed, at first glance, too aristocratic. He spoke with something like a slight British accent that sounded haughty and conceited. They wondered how someone with his background could connect with common farmers and laborers.

Now they wanted a weak federal government because they didn't want the government regulating *them*.

The Republican Party—Lincoln's anti-slavery, pro-industry party—was torn between its two original missions. Was it mostly a pro-labor party or was it mostly pro-industry?

Republicans like Theodore Roosevelt believed the party should continue its anti-slavery tradition of helping the oppressed, in this case, the laborers. Others disagreed and said the Republicans were the party of business owners, and their task was to help make industry more prosperous, which in their view, meant opposing labor unions.

On the other hand, there was magic in his last name, connecting him to one of the most energetic and revered figures of the era. His wealth was also an obvious bonus. He'd be able to pay his way, and hopefully help out the local party. The Democrats agreed to nominate him for a state senate seat representing

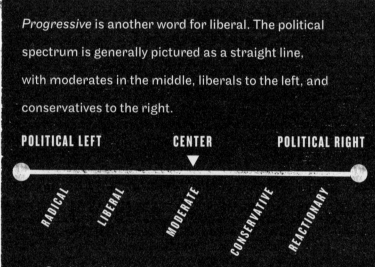

Progressive is another word for liberal. The political spectrum is generally pictured as a straight line, with moderates in the middle, liberals to the left, and conservatives to the right.

POLITICAL LEFT   CENTER   POLITICAL RIGHT

RADICAL   LIBERAL   MODERATE   CONSERVATIVE   REACTIONARY

On the political left side of the spectrum, liberals are comfortable with change, and look for changes that they believe will improve society. Radicals want to bring about swift changes, looking eagerly ahead to what they believe will be a better world. On the political right, conservatives are less comfortable with change.

Putnam, Columbia, and Dutchess Counties, which included Hyde Park. Nobody thought he'd win. With the exception of the small city of Poughkeepsie, the area was heavily Republican. Only once in New York history had those counties ever sent a Democrat to the state senate.

They prefer stability and the status quo. Reactionaries long nostalgically for the past—a time they believe things used to be better. Those in the middle, moderates, shy away from extreme views.

Liberals and radicals welcome change partly because they tend to see history as evolving and improving. Reactionaries have the opposite view— they believe things are getting worse, so they want to retreat to the past and restore the order of how things used to be.

During Lincoln's time, the liberals and radicals trying to bring about change had been anti-slavery Republicans, while the conservatives and reactionaries trying to hold on to the status quo or trying to go back to the old ways had been the Democrats. By the early twentieth century, the parties were shifting.

Franklin first sought the blessing of his famous cousin. Teddy Roosevelt would have liked for Franklin to run as a Republican or independent, but he gave his blessing to Franklin, saying he'd always liked the boy.

Franklin devised the perfect campaign pitch for the district. Both parties were then ruled by party bosses who called the shots from behind the scenes. Franklin declared himself against *all* party bosses and in favor of more democracy and what he called clean government, which allowed him to be in favor of something universally seen as good while sidestepping the controversial question of whether government should be large or small. He declared himself a progressive Democrat.

✳ ✳ ✳ ✳ ✳ ✳ ✳ ✳ ✳ ✳ ✳ ✳ ✳ ✳ ✳

On September 23, 1910, Eleanor gave birth to their fourth child, a boy who they named Elliott after Eleanor's father. Two weeks later, at the annual session of the Dutchess County Democratic Committee in Poughkeepsie, Franklin accepted the nomination for state senator. In his acceptance speech, he told the committee, "I am pledged to no man; I am influenced by no special interest, and so I shall remain." He denounced his opponent, incumbent John F. Schlosser, as being a member of "that little ring of Republican politicians who have done so much to prevent progress and good government."

Franklin hired a driver and a bright red open car. He decorated the car with flags and streamers and campaigned energetically through the farm areas, declaring himself a friend to farmers.

Franklin at a campaign stop in Dutchess County, New York, 1910

In a one-on-one conversation he could come across as a bit too aristocratic, but in front of a crowd he exuded charm and self-confidence. He exploited his famous last name by announcing himself "dee-lighted" by everything—the weather, his prospects, the size of crowds. He spoke to people from front porches and in dairy barns, anywhere he could assemble a crowd. He addressed people as "my friends." He never lost his good humor. "When I see you again," he told a group at a crossroads rally, "I will be your State Senator." A farmer grumbled, "Like h— you will." Franklin merrily joined in the laughter before gunning off with his driver to the next stop.

His opponent, Schlosser, attacked Franklin's aristocratic roots and dandified appearance. Franklin responded by attacking Schlosser's subservience to Republican Party bosses in Albany. With characteristic exuberance, Franklin later described the campaign by saying, "I had a particularly disagreeable opponent. He called me names . . . the names I called him were worse than the names he called me. So we had a joyous campaign." It's possible he did indeed enjoy the fight. It's also possible that he responded to the attacks of his opponents the same way he responded to bullies during his first year at Groton: He protected himself by pretending to have fun.

On election night, Franklin waited for the returns at Hyde Park with Sara, Eleanor, and a houseful of friends and supporters. Democrats did well in all regions of the United States, and particularly well in New York, gaining majorities in both houses of the legislature.

Franklin—to the surprise of many—won a two-year term as a state senator.

✶ ✶ ✶ ✶ ✶ ✶ ✶ ✶ ✶ ✶ ✶ ✶ ✶ ✶ ✶

Franklin rented a large and comfortable house on Albany's quiet, cobbled Upper State Street. The rent was more than three times his salary as a state senator, and more than he and Eleanor could afford with their trust fund income, but he gave the money no thought. He knew Sara would contribute whatever additional money he needed. His extravagant home, fully staffed with nannies, maids, and a butler, was not lost on his new colleagues and political opponents, many of whom had fought their way up from poverty and resented those they considered elite. Eleanor felt they should live within their own incomes, but Franklin brushed aside Eleanor's concerns.

He threw himself into his new job. The first task of the state senate was to select the United States Senator from New York. (Senators at the time were selected by state legislatures.) The Republican Party bosses and the Democrat party bosses came to an agreement between themselves that a man named William "Blue-Eyed Billy" Sheehan should become New York's senator.

Franklin challenged the decision on the grounds that party

bosses selecting senators was undemocratic. He joined with other Democrats to relentlessly batter Sheehan's reputation, until at last, feeling pummeled, Sheehan withdrew his nomination. The candidate eventually selected was a Manhattan lawyer named James O'Gorman, a compromise candidate with wider appeal. Franklin earned a state-wide reputation for being willing to take on the party bosses. "You know," he said later, "I was an awfully mean cuss when I first went into politics."

✳ ✳ ✳ ✳ ✳ ✳ ✳ ✳ ✳ ✳ ✳ ✳ ✳ ✳ ✳

F ranklin soon mastered the art of local politics. He came to understand how even the simplest farm bill touched

By the early twentieth century, the problems with state legislatures selecting the United States senators was becoming clear: Because senators were often chosen by party bosses or a few powerful men, the senators were accused of acting as puppets for the rich and powerful instead of representing the people. In 1911, as a result of the battle in New York over the senator from the state and multiple strands of society: merchants, railroads, canneries, and—of course—the individual farmers themselves. He learned that if he wanted to survive as a politician, he could not fight the party bosses all the time. There were times to fight, but sometimes it was better to compromise, or simply give in.

He also discovered that being a pedigreed member of what his mother approvingly called American aristocracy was not helpful in the Democratic Party. He received lessons in how to conduct himself from an unlikely source, an Albany newspaperman named Louis McHenry Howe, who advised Franklin to drop his aristocratic mannerism and expressions. Franklin and Howe soon became close friends, with Howe taking on the role of chief advisor.

similar quarrels in other states, the House of Representatives and Senate passed the Seventeenth Amendment requiring senators to be elected by direct vote of the people. On April 8, 1913, three-quarters of the states ratified the proposed amendment, and it became part of the Constitution. In contrast, the members of the House of Representatives have always been chosen by direct vote of the people.

Neither Eleanor nor Sara liked Howe, finding him ill-mannered and unappealing. "That dirty little man," Sara called him. Howe, indeed, was coarse and bluntly outspoken, having worked himself up from poverty to become an influential reporter. Franklin and Howe seemed as different as could be. Franklin was guarded and careful and aristocratic. But Howe recog-

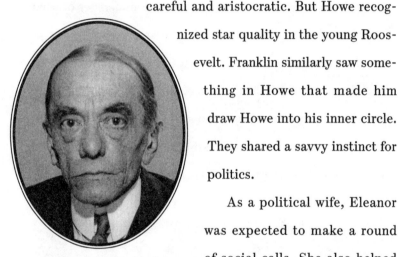

Louis McHenry Howe

nized star quality in the young Roos-evelt. Franklin similarly saw some-thing in Howe that made him draw Howe into his inner circle. They shared a savvy instinct for politics.

As a political wife, Eleanor was expected to make a round of social calls. She also helped Franklin clarify his thoughts by listening closely and asking questions, as she had seen her aunt Edith do with Uncle Theodore. She went to the senate gallery to listen to debates and she read political newspapers. Later Franklin said that was the beginning of her "political sagacity."

She listened closely to how people talked about Franklin

and discovered that many people viewed him as a lightweight, a fool, and a spoiled rich boy interested only in publicity. According to one observer: "He had a youthful lack of humility, a streak of self-righteousness, and a deafness to the hopes, fears, and aspirations which are the common lot." Eleanor told him he needed to sound more assured, he needed to be more precise with facts, and he needed to be more concerned about the real needs of his constituents. Franklin heeded her advice.

Franklin always loved interacting with people. Now, thrown into the quagmire of local politics, he became better at negotiating and wrangling. He learned the power of language and the importance of choosing the right word. For example, he was in favor of regulations to protect the environment, but learned that if he said "government regulation" lots of people would shrink in horror. "But if we call the same process 'cooperation,'" he explained, "these same old fogeys will cry out 'well done.'"

During his second year in the New York State Senate, a constitutional amendment was proposed to the New York legislature granting women the right to vote in New York. Franklin considered the matter, then declared himself in favor of women voting.

The woman's suffrage bill failed. The women activists in New York, though, vowed to gather more signatures and submit the bill again.

★ ★ ★ ★ ★ ★ ★ ★ ★ ★ ★ ★ ★ ★

When it came time to run for reelection, Franklin again threw himself into the campaign with energy and optimism. As with his first race, he ran on a pro-labor, anti-party boss platform.

That was also the year of a presidential election. Theodore Roosevelt was no longer president. He tried but failed to secure the Republican nomination. The nomination went to the more conservative, pro-business, anti-labor candidate, William Howard Taft. The problem for Teddy Roosevelt was that the Republican Party was turning into an anti-labor party, but he couldn't bring himself to join the Democrats. So he formed a new party, the Progressive Party and—following the footsteps of Abraham Lincoln—said, "We are for liberty, but we are for the liberty of the oppressed."

The Democratic nominee was Woodrow Wilson, governor of New Jersey. Wilson, like Teddy Roosevelt, was in favor of legislation protecting workers and guaranteeing safe working conditions and living wages. Wilson said, "I am fighting, not for the man who has made good, but for the man who is going to make good—the man who is knocking and fighting at the closed doors of opportunity." Thus in their position on labor versus business tycoons, there was not much difference between Theodore Roosevelt's Progressive Party and the Democrats. In their position on race, though, they were worlds apart: The Democrats remained the party of white Southerners who still clung to the ideals of the old Confederacy. They envisioned laborers as white. Roosevelt's party, though, sought to promote the interests of *all* oppressed people.

Shortly after Franklin launched his own campaign for reelection, both he and Eleanor came down with typhoid and were confined to bed. Not about to be deterred, Franklin enlisted Louis McHenry Howe's help. Howe took up the work of the campaign, publishing ads in newspapers, sending thousands of personalized letters from Franklin to farmers throughout the district. Howe focused on persuading specific groups of voters. For example, after clearing his plans with Franklin, he promised fishermen that license fees would be lowered and apple growers that Franklin would introduce a bill to standardize the size of their barrels.

Woodrow Wilson at his desk, 1913

When the votes were counted on election night, Franklin won a second term as New York state senator. Democrat Woodrow Wilson won the presidency, with Teddy Roosevelt coming in second, and the Republican incumbent, Taft, trailing in third place.

★ ★ ★ ★ ★ ★ ★ ★ ★ ★ ★ ★ ★ ★

Franklin kicked off his second term by introducing an impressive number of bills to benefit farmers, including those Howe had promised during the campaign. With a Democratic president about to take office, however, Franklin had his eye on a bigger job. In January, he and Eleanor traveled to Washington, D.C., to attend Wilson's inauguration. He had a private meeting with Wilson, during which he told Wilson he wanted the job of assistant secretary of the navy.

Wilson had already offered the position of secretary of the navy to a man named Josephus Daniels. On the morning of the inauguration, Franklin spied Daniels in the crowded lobby of the

Willard Hotel. They spoke briefly. At
the end of the conversation, Franklin had in hand his dream job
offer: the post of assistant secretary of the navy—the job that,
years earlier, he'd said would be
his second step on the road to the
presidency.

Josephus Daniels, 1913

As Franklin later told the
story, his conversation with Dan-
iels went like this: Franklin said to Daniels that all his life he
had loved ships and studied the navy. Daniels then asked, "How
would you like to come to Washington as Assistant Secretary of
the Navy?" Franklin beamed in response, and said, "How would
I like it? I'd like it bully well. It would please me better than
anything in the world." Presumably there was more to the story,
but this was all Franklin had to say about it.

Daniels later said that he offered Franklin the job to achieve
regional balance on his staff. He wanted a well-connected New
Yorker. He also recognized that Franklin was "our kind of liberal."

New York Senator Elihu Root, a savvy political com-
mentator, warned Daniels that Franklin would try to take

over. "You know the Roosevelts, don't you?" he said. "Whenever a Roosevelt rides, he wishes to ride in front."

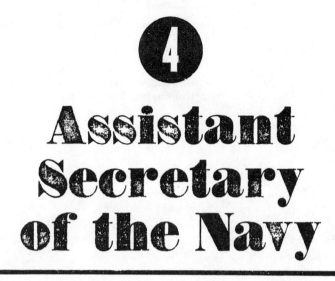

4

Assistant Secretary of the Navy

"Happiness lies in the joy of achievement,
in the thrill of creative effort."

— *Franklin Delano Roosevelt*

n March, Franklin resigned his post as state senator. On March 17, 1913, he was sworn in as assistant secretary of the navy. He was thirty-one years old. It was also his eighth wedding anniversary. Eleanor was in Albany with their children. "My only regret," he wrote to her from his new desk, "is that you couldn't have been here with me." He spent his first six months on the job living in hotels in Washington, D.C., while his family remained in Albany.

The Department of the Navy managed a large budget and

Franklin, as assistant secretary of the navy, attended the launching of the USS *Tennessee*, a battleship.

maintained a fleet of battleships. The secretary of the navy had only one assistant, which offered Franklin the chance to get a crash course in government bureaucracy. He loved the job. In particular, he loved being part of the pomp and ceremony of the navy.

Daniels was stunned when Franklin quickly and expertly seized control of the operations, all the while smiling as if the task were nothing. "I get my fingers into everything," Franklin said cheerfully, "and there's no law against it."

The thousands of department employees belonged to a labor union. Franklin's strategy was to prevent disputes with labor by telling the union leaders, "I want you all to feel that you can come to me at any time in my office and we can talk matters over." They did, and disputes were worked out amiably. It was soon evident that the Navy Department, unlike other federal departments, would not have conflicts with organized labor.

Government work often extended into evenings at dinners and parties. Deals were made at social events. Friendships and liaisons were formed. The nation's most respected politicians and leaders attended Washington, D.C., social events. Franklin threw himself into Washington nightlife, and was thus able to make himself known to Democratic party leaders at the highest levels. One observer remembered him as "brilliant, lovable, and somewhat happy-go-lucky . . . always amusing, always the life of the party." He presented himself as a progressive Democrat. With the Republican Party becoming more conservative, he grandly invited all progressive Republicans to abandon their party and join the Democrats.

At the end of the summer, Eleanor and the children joined him. Anna was then six, James was five, and Elliott a toddler of two. Eleanor brought a car and chauffeur, a nurse, governess, and four additional household staff. They all moved into a four-story brick home owned by Teddy Roosevelt's sister, Eleanor's aunt Bamie, located a convenient six blocks from the Navy Department. Having his family with him didn't change Franklin's lifestyle. He spent much of his time away from home, working, socializing, and traveling on navy business. Sara was proud that her son was in a "*very* big job." She wrote him letters offering practical advice, such as "Try not to write your signature too small as it gets a cramped look and is not distinct. So many public men have awful signatures, and so unreadable."

Eleanor, meanwhile, followed the advice of one of her aunts, who told her she was supposed to pay social calls to official wives—the wives of Supreme Court Justices, cabinet members, and members of Congress. Eleanor sometimes made as many as thirty personal visits each day, rarely staying longer than six minutes. As part of her duties, she attended what felt like an endless round of formal dinners. Being a Washington, D.C., official wife was much more demanding than an Albany, New York, official wife. The shy and sensitive Eleanor found the round of activity tedious, and not at all to her liking. To make sure she was being useful, she acted as a scout for Franklin, looking for allies and keeping careful notes for him.

✶ ✶ ✶ ✶ ✶ ✶ ✶ ✶ ✶ ✶ ✶ ✶ ✶ ✶ ✶

President Wilson enacted a pro-labor pro-farmer agenda: He supported a bill regulating child labor, which didn't pass, and he made loans widely available to farmers. To please his white Southern base, he also enacted a racist agenda. Black appointees were discharged and replaced by whites. Federal government staff and laborers were segregated by race. W. E. B. Du Bois, a black leader who had supported Wilson because of his stance on labor, lamented the "personal insult and humiliation" being heaped on innocent blacks as a result of the government's racial segregation.

At the end of the Civil War, the Fourteenth Amendment was added to the Constitution guaranteeing all citizens "equal treatment of the law." By the late nineteenth century, though, the former Confederate states had regained enough power to push back by enacting laws depriving blacks of freedom, including laws making it difficult for blacks to vote.

These laws sparked anger and resistance. To put an end to the conflicts, the United States Supreme Court, consisting mostly of justices sympathetic to the former Confederacy, stepped into the fray. The court upheld voter restriction laws on the grounds that the states should have autonomy in these matters. In a case called *Plessy v. Ferguson*, the Supreme Court even declared segregation constitutional holding that as long as separate facilities were equal, they didn't violate the equal protection clause of the Fourteenth Amendment.

★ ★ ★ ★ ★ ★ ★ ★ ★ ★ ★ ★ ★ ★

n June 28, 1914 something happened in Bosnia, a small kingdom in Southeastern Europe, that would have a

Once the Supreme Court interprets the Constitution, there are only two ways to reverse the decision: 1. Persuade the Supreme Court to overrule itself, which rarely happens, and moreover, was not going to happen given the pro-Confederacy leanings of many of the Supreme Court Justices, or 2. Amend the Constitution, a long and laborious process that requires two-thirds of the states to agree. It was clear that two-thirds of the states would not agree to end segregation, so reversing *Plessy v. Ferguson* by amending the Constitution was also impossible at that time.

In 1909, a group of black and white activists established the National Association for the Advancement of Colored People, known as the NAACP. One of the NAACP's goals was to work on ending racial segregation. In time, the organization would grow powerful enough to challenge the Supreme Court's decision in *Plessy v. Ferguson*. But such a challenge was still many decades in the future.

far-reaching impact on the United States, and indeed, most of the world.

Bosnia was then under the rule of the Austro-Hungarian

Empire (Austria-Hungary), a vast empire that controlled much of Europe. For years, tensions had been simmering in Europe as the Austrians, in alliance with Germany, grew stronger and stronger.

On that fateful day in June, an assassin killed an Austrian archduke, Franz Ferdinand, and his wife, Sophie, while they were visiting Sarajevo, the capital of Bosnia. The assassin—who was of Bosnian and Serbian heritage—believed that killing Ferdinand would help Bosnia win independence. The Austrians, enraged over the killing, blamed the Serbian government. Exactly one month after the assassination, Austria-Hungary declared war on Serbia. Imperial Russia—wanting to limit Austria-Hungary's power—immediately sided with Serbia. Two days later, Germany honored its alliance with Austria-Hungary and jumped into the war on Austria's side by declaring war on Russia.

Thus began the Great War, later called World War I.

Franklin was in Pennsylvania on navy business when the news broke. He received a telegram summoning him back to Washington, D.C. On the train, he wrote Eleanor a brief note telling her what happened, adding, "A complete smashup is inevitable." He understood that the war would escalate and upset the precarious power balance in Europe, and because tensions had been simmering for years, there was no way to avert the conflict. "The best that can be expected," he predicted, "is a sharp, complete and quick victory by one side, a most unlikely occurrence, or a speedy realization of impending bankruptcy to all, and a cessation of mutual consent, but this too I think unlikely."

When Franklin arrived back in Washington, he went straight to the Department of the Navy. "As I expected," he said, "I found everything asleep and apparently oblivious to the fact that the most terrible drama in history was about to be enacted." Daniels, secretary of the navy, was mired in sadness over the fact that the "gentlemen" ruling Europe could not work out their differences without resorting to war. Hadn't civilization advanced beyond such barbarity? Franklin described Daniels as "bewildered by it all, very sweet but very sad."

Franklin had no patience for sadness at such a time. He believed the moment called for action. He thought Wilson and Daniels should prepare the United States for an emergency. He also believed the United States must make sure Austria-Hungary and Germany didn't grow too powerful and swallow up the rest of Europe.

The Germans knew the French would jump in on Russia's side, so shortly after declaring war on Russia, Germany ordered

FDR flashing a
smile, 1915

Belgium to provide safe passage for German armies en route to France. Belgium refused. So two days later, on August 3, 1914, Germany declared war on France. The next day, Germany invaded Belgium. On August 4, England declared war on Germany.

President Wilson committed the United States to complete neutrality. He ordered the navy to watch the coasts, but gave orders nobody was to make any statements about the war. The prevailing opinion in the United States was that Europe's war was none of America's business.

✳ ✳ ✳ ✳ ✳ ✳ ✳ ✳ ✳ ✳ ✳ ✳ ✳ ✳ ✳

Franklin, who'd been keeping his eye on New York politics, saw an opportunity to run for U.S. senator from New York. Franklin announced himself as a candidate on August 13, 1914. Four days later, August 17, 1914, Eleanor gave birth to another son, Franklin Roosevelt Jr., bringing the number of children up to four, one daughter and three sons. Eleanor therefore stayed on the sidelines during the campaign.

Franklin's bid for U.S. Senator from New York hit a snag when the New York Democratic Party bosses ran another Democrat against him in the primaries. This caught him by surprise.

He hadn't expected a Democratic opponent. He went to New York and tried to campaign, but having been away, with his mind on the navy and the war in Europe, he didn't have a good grasp on the issues just then facing the state, and he wasn't prepared to take on the party bosses. When he lost, he insisted he was not disappointed. Cheerfully he told the press it had been a "good fight." Daniels, who by then had more insight into Franklin's character, understood that Franklin was more disappointed and hurt than he let on.

✷ ✷ ✷ ✷ ✷ ✷ ✷ ✷ ✷ ✷ ✷ ✷ ✷ ✷ ✷

President Wilson's policy of keeping the United States neutral received a blow on May 7, 1915, when the Germans torpedoed a British passenger ocean liner, the RMS *Lusitania*—the largest and fastest ship in the North Atlantic run. The ship sank within eighteen minutes, killing 1,198 people, leaving 761 survivors. Of the dead, 128 were Americans. The Germans defended the attack by saying the ship was carrying weapons— which was true, the *Lusitania* was transporting munitions for war. The Germans, therefore, claimed that the ship was a legitimate military target. They also said the British were to blame for the civilian deaths for hiding weapons behind civilians.

Lusitania coming into port, possibly in New York (between 1907–1915)

The sinking of the *Lusitania* helped change the tide of public opinion in the United States. Newspapers railed against the "wanton murder" of helpless civilians. Wilson managed to calm the nation, but tensions were high. Wilson gave Daniels orders to make sure the navy was ready for war, should it come. Franklin therefore spent his days working on a plan for expanding the navy's capabilities, including creating a naval reserve, and the immediate construction of 176 ships at a total cost of $600 million. He was supposed to do all of this while making it appear routine and not in preparation for war. He understood that "The President does not want to rattle the sword."

★ ★ ★ ★ ★ ★ ★ ★ ★ ★ ★ ★ ★ ★ ★

On March 13, 1916, Franklin went out to dinner, leaving Eleanor, who was expecting another baby anytime, at home. He returned after his dinner engagement to discover that another son had been born. Eleanor and the baby were doing fine. Franklin was now the father of five children. He and Eleanor named the baby John Aspinwall Roosevelt. Eleanor was thus excused from the usual duties of official wives. "For ten years," she later explained, "I was always just getting over having a baby or about to have one, and so my occupations were considerably restricted during this period."

That was also an election year. President Wilson's decision to stay out of the war was popular with most Americans, as was his pro-labor agenda. When the votes were counted in November, he earned 49.4 percent of the popular vote, while Charles Evans Hughes, his opponent, won 46.2 percent. For Franklin, this meant four more years as assistant secretary of the navy.

★　★　★　★　★　★　★　★　★　★　★　★　★　★　★

The war was going badly for Germany and the Austro-Hungarian Empire, and the Germans were getting nervous. The British navy was patrolling the North Sea, preventing cargo ships from reaching Germany and the Austro-Hungarian Empire. Britain, on the other hand, was freely trading with neutral countries. The Germany military chiefs wanted to declare the area around the British Isles a war zone, meaning that all merchant ships, including those from neutral countries, would be vulnerable to attack by the German navy. The Germans called their plan "unrestricted submarine warfare." For a long time, Emperor Wilhelm II, of Germany, and his officials refused to allow it, partly because they understood such tactics would force the United States into the war.

In early 1917, the German military commanders persuaded the German officials that without drastic measures, Germany would be badly defeated. The officials gave their approval for unrestricted submarine warfare. The German military flashed warnings that any vessels in the waters around Great Britain were subject to attack.

On February 3, 1917 the Germans boarded the SS *Housatonic,* an American ocean liner carrying wheat and flour to England. The German captain explained that he had orders to sink the ship because it was carrying food to a belligerent enemy. He ordered all persons from the ship to evacuate via lifeboats. When everyone was removed, the Germans torpedoed and sank the ship.

Wilson agonized for a few months, and then concluded he had no choice: The United States must enter the Great War.

The
Great War

"Courage is not the absence of fear,
but rather the assessment that something
else is more important than fear."

— *Franklin Delano Roosevelt*

n April 2, 1917, backed by his unanimous cabinet, President Wilson addressed Congress and asked for a declaration of war. (Under the Constitution, the president is commander in chief of the armed forces, but Congress must declare war.)

With the United States in the war, Franklin was busier than ever. He had to step up naval construction, organize recruits and reserves, and plan the deployment of ships. He was one of the few members of Wilson's administration who spoke fluent French, so he was often asked to meet with French emissaries who came to Washington, D.C. He relentlessly pushed the slow-moving Daniels as if Daniels were a subordinate instead of his boss. A typical memo, addressed "Dear Mr. Daniels," gave orders:

> *Do please get through two vital things today. 1) Get that Interior Building or give it to War Dept. & let us take latter's space here 2) Authorize calling out Naval Militia and Reserve. It is essential to get them if we are to go ahead. Roosevelt.*

Eleanor's life also changed. With the war on, the "women in Washington paid no more [social] calls," and instead, organized "to meet the unusual demand of wartime." Anna, James, and Elliott now attended day schools and the younger children were cared for by nannies, so Eleanor joined women's groups to help with the war effort. She ran one of the Red Cross canteens at Union Station, a public plaza at the foot of Capitol Hill. Wearing a khaki uniform, she handed out sandwiches, newspapers, and cups of coffee to trainloads of soldiers on their way to army camps. She worked tirelessly, often long past midnight. The work gave her a renewed energy, and an exhilarating sense of purpose.

Women had contributed to each of America's wars, but this time was different. Because the women's rights movement had been building in America for decades, the women's groups were already organized and thus able to mobilize quickly and efficiently. They were so professional and efficient, the men took notice. The armed forces decided, for the first time, to allow women other than nurses to enlist. Women served primarily in clerical positions, but they worked alongside men, doing the same work for the same pay.

Eleanor was juggling so much, between managing the house, overseeing the upbringing of the children, and volunteering upwards of twelve-hour days, she needed her own secretary. She hired a part-time secretary, Lucy Mercer, a girl from a well-connected family who needed paying work because her family had fallen on difficult financial times. Lucy was pleasant, competent, and wonderful with the children. They adored her. She could step into Eleanor's place when Eleanor was off volunteering. Lucy saw what needed to be done, and did it without being asked. Eleanor came to rely on her.

When Franklin was in Washington, D.C., he spent his days working, and his nights at parties and social events. During the war years, Washington nightlife was glamorous and glittering, and Franklin wanted to unwind after a stressful day. He went out more often, and stayed out later. By this time, nobody thought of Franklin

Lucy Mercer, circa 1913

as a hayseed or a feather duster. While he still hid his sharp mind behind a jovial smile, it was clear to people that he was, in fact, competent and far-sighted. He'd also matured into a strikingly good-looking man. His cousins now described him as "debonair." He enjoyed flirting while he was out. He often flirted with Lucy Mercer, whom he frequently saw at evening events.

Eleanor, in contrast, became more serious, avoiding parties altogether to volunteer in hospitals. She was so focused on her work she didn't even notice hardships. One day, while preparing for the arrival of wounded soldiers during one of the steamiest heat waves of the summer of 1918, she cut her finger to the bone. She bandaged her finger, kept working, and bore the scar for the rest of her life.

She took a personal interest in each of the wounded soldiers. She brought them fresh flowers, candy, and newspapers. Listening to their stories, and learning about lives so different from her own, filled her with deep compassion and gave her a new awareness of the world. For the first time she questioned the ideas and values upon which she had been raised, including the ideas about the American aristocracy that Sara held so dear. It dawned on Eleanor for the first time that the notion of an elite class of people—white, well educated, Protestant, and wealthy— was outdated and had no place in the modern world.

Soldiers of the 308th Infantry Regiment at Camp Upton, New York (1917–1918)

The Great War

Franklin had predicted the war would be a smashup, and it was. Modern technology had created highly destructive weapons including hand grenades and machine guns. Airplanes were still crude, made of canvas, wood, and wire, but the Germans figured out how to arm them with machine guns, which allowed them to gun down advancing armies. The new technologically advanced defensive weapons made traditional ways of penetrating enemy lines impossible. Thousands of lives were lost simply to claim a few hundred yards of earth. Before the end of the war, sixteen million soldiers and civilians would be killed. The death toll was frighteningly high partly because military leaders were slow to adapt traditional methods of warfare to modern technology.

Russia soon found itself in deep trouble. By early 1917, more than 1.7 million Russians had died in the war, and another five million were wounded. Russian soldiers were largely drawn from the lower classes of peasants and laborers. Tensions had been brewing in Russia for years, with widespread resentment of the extravagant lifestyle of the ruling monarchs, Czar Nicholas and Czarina Alexandra. When it became clear that the wealthy sent the poor laborers to be slaughtered for a war that nobody understood, resentment erupted in one of the most explosive and far-reaching single events in modern European history: The Russian Revolution.

The Russian revolutionaries called themselves Communists and claimed their inspiration from the teachings of Karl Marx, a philosopher who argued that laborers were being exploited by wealthy factory owners. Marx said laborers should own the fruits of their own labor. He predicted a perfect future in which workers ruled themselves without kings or emperors. The revolutionaries, fired up by the teachings of Marx, demanded that the czar

Armed soldiers carry a banner reading Communism, Moscow, October 1917

abdicate and hand over power to the people. The czar responded with harsh measures to put down the rebellion. Russian soldiers in large numbers deserted the army to join the revolution.

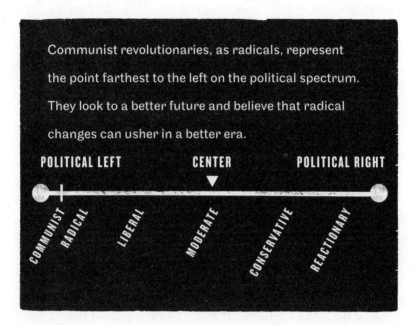

Communist revolutionaries, as radicals, represent the point farthest to the left on the political spectrum. They look to a better future and believe that radical changes can usher in a better era.

POLITICAL LEFT   CENTER   POLITICAL RIGHT

COMMUNIST   RADICAL   LIBERAL   MODERATE   CONSERVATIVE   REACTIONARY

In March of 1918, Russia, unable to fight Germany because of internal turmoil, signed a peace treaty ceding a large portion of their territory to Germany. The United States, France, England, and their allies were now fighting the Germans and Austrians on their own.

By July, the Russian revolutionaries had seized control of the imperial government and executed the czar, czarina, and their children. The revolutionaries next seized all private property in the name of the people. Unfortunately, the revolutionary government that replaced the czar failed to live up to Karl Marx's ideal state in which workers were happy, productive, and free.

Instead of the workers owning the products of their own labor, the government owned and controlled all of the nation's industries and resources. Communism thus came to be associated with a strong central government. In theory the government was supposed to redistribute wealth and power to the people, but this didn't happen: The government retained complete control and instituted a totalitarian regime—meaning a few people made the rules without input from the people. Most ordinary Russians found the new Communist regime as oppressive as the previous one.

In 1922, the leaders of the revolution renamed Russia the Union of Soviet Socialist Republics, commonly referred to as the Soviet Union.

✴ ✴ ✴ ✴ ✴ ✴ ✴ ✴ ✴ ✴ ✴ ✴ ✴ ✴ ✴

I n July of 1918, the same month the Czar and his family were executed in Russia, Franklin boarded a destroyer, the USS *Dyer*, under secret orders, which meant neither Sara nor Eleanor

Franklin in Pauillac, France, stepping off of a seaplane, 1918

could see him off at the dock. He was going to Europe to take care of navy business and see the progress of the war for himself. Once there, he traveled through much of Europe, including France, England, Scotland, and Italy, visiting battlefields and dignitaries. He was received at Buckingham Palace, and met Winston Churchill, a minister of the British aristocracy who then held the government post of master of munitions, overseeing the production and distribution of munitions for the war effort.

Later Franklin said of his 1918 travels through Europe:

I have seen war on land and sea. I have seen blood running from the wounded. I have seen men coughing out their gassed lungs. I have seen the dead in the mud. I have seen cities destroyed . . . I have seen the agony of mothers and wives. I hate war.

✷　✷　✷　✷　✷　✷　✷　✷　✷　✷　✷　✷　✷

In September, while he was heading home, a deadly bout of flu broke out on his ship. Many of the crew and officers died and were buried at sea. Franklin also fell ill, and ended up with double pneumonia. When his ship arrived in New York on September 19, both Sara and Eleanor, having heard that he was sick, were at the dock to meet him. They'd left the children in Hyde Park. Franklin was so weak he was carried off the ship to a waiting ambulance and taken to Sara's house. He was lifted up the stairs by four hospital orderlies.

Later, Eleanor was in a guest bedroom unpacking Franklin's suitcase when she found a neat packet of love letters tied with a ribbon. They were written to him from Lucy Mercer. How much—or what—she read, we don't know, but from those letters, she learned that Lucy and her husband had fallen in love. She also learned that during many of Franklin's evenings out, he had been with Lucy—a deeply humiliating realization. "The bottom dropped out of my own particular world," she later wrote to a friend, "and I faced myself, my surroundings, my world honestly for the first time. I really grew up that year."

She gave Franklin an ultimatum: If he wanted to be free to spend time with other women, she would be happy to divorce him. But she would not remain his wife if he dallied with other women. Franklin took a while to reach a decision. What galled Eleanor—and part of what she had difficulty forgiving later—was how long it took him to decide.

When Sara caught wind of what was going on, she threw her weight behind Eleanor, warning Franklin that if he left his wife and children for another woman and smeared the family name with scandal, she would immediately cut him off and he would not inherit a penny of her fortune. Louis Howe, too, sternly warned Franklin to stop seeing Lucy unless he wanted to put an end to his political career.

Eleanor brought the children to their home in Washington, D.C. Meanwhile, Franklin went to Hyde Park to recuperate from his illness. After he recovered, he and Eleanor were reunited on October 18, 1918, in Washington. Franklin tried to repair the damage he had done to his marriage. He became more solicitous of Eleanor's feelings and tried to be more attentive. He played a more active role in the family: He helped Anna with her math homework, and he took Elliott for horseback rides. He became fiercely protective of Eleanor, never allowing anyone to say anything negative about her.

But Eleanor—betrayed and deeply wounded—would never be the same. Her childhood illusions of love were shattered. For the remainder of her life, she had difficulty talking about Lucy, even to her closest friends. "I can forgive," she told one friend, "but I can never forget."

★ ★ ★ ★ ★ ★ ★ ★ ★ ★ ★ ★ ★ ★ ★

In September of 1918, the same month Eleanor found Lucy Mercer's letters, President Woodrow Wilson took a momentous step toward women's rights in America. He'd always been indifferent to the cause of woman's suffrage, but seeing the impressive contribution women made to the war effort, he changed his mind and heeded the pleas of the women activists. "We have made partners of the women in this war," he said, "shall we admit them only to a partnership of suffering and sacrifice and toil and not to a partnership of privilege and right?" He asked the Senate to pass an amendment guaranteeing women the right to vote. Congress heeded his call and drafted the amendment, which stated simply that:

> *The right of citizens of the United States to vote shall not be denied or abridged by the United States or by any state on account of sex.*
>
> *Congress shall have power to enforce this article by appropriate legislation.*

In the spring of 1919, the House and Senate passed what would become the Nineteenth Amendment, also known as the Susan B. Anthony Amendment. On August 18, 1920, Tennessee became the thirty-sixth state to ratify the amendment, making the Nineteenth Amendment part of the United States Constitution.

✶ ✶ ✶ ✶ ✶ ✶ ✶ ✶ ✶ ✶ ✶ ✶ ✶ ✶ ✶

Early in November of 1918, the German generals told the German emperor that they could no longer fight. They didn't have enough supplies or soldiers. At 11:00 a.m., on the eleventh day of the eleventh month of 1918, World War I ended when Germany signed an agreement to end the fighting.

Franklin had business to tie up in Europe. Eleanor

accompanied him on the trip. They were at sea on their way to Paris when they learned from a radio announcement that Theodore Roosevelt died in his sleep after what they had thought was a minor illness. "My cousin's death was in every way a great shock," Franklin later told Daniels, "for we'd heard just before leaving that he was better." Grieving, Franklin and Eleanor continued on their trip, as planned.

They found Paris devastated, but in a celebratory mood with the war over. Franklin dismantled the American naval establishment in Europe, and attended peace conferences with President Wilson, who was working to form an organization called the League of Nations. Wilson hoped such a league would prevent future wars, but the idea never caught on with the American voters, who feared that such alliances would draw the United States into future wars.

✸ ✸ ✸ ✸ ✸ ✸ ✸ ✸ ✸ ✸ ✸ ✸ ✸ ✸ ✸

efore World War I, America's greatest military victory against a foreign enemy was in 1815, when General Andrew Jackson defended America from a British attack in the Battle of New Orleans. Now the United States had helped defeat and dismantle Europe's most powerful empires. America had entered the war late, and saw no fighting on American soil, so America emerged with a robust economy. With the continent of Europe devastated, the United States emerged for the first time as a global economic leader.

The word *economy* refers to the systems of wealth creation and structure of resources of a nation or region. The economy is usually measured in terms of production or use of goods and services. In a strong economy, there is a market for all kinds of goods and services, enabling farmers or factory owners to sell what they produce, encouraging more production and creating more jobs. In a weak economy, the opposite happens. There are few jobs available, which means people have less money to spend, which in turn, depresses production and sale of goods and demand for services.

The fighting was over, but new troubles were already brewing in Europe. The Austro-Hungarian Empire was broken apart, and the ruling family ousted. The German Empire, too, was dismantled and the German emperor abdicated his power. The ruling order of continental Europe was smashed, and much of the aristocracy toppled. Chaos filled the void. New nations were haphazardly carved out of the disintegrated empires, occasionally lumping together into a single nation lands with separate histories, cultures, and even languages.

Like the soldiers in Russia, soldiers throughout Europe who survived and returned home were no longer content to have second-class status. The wounded refused to be left to starve. There was generally no government aid to help those who had been wounded in a war. Like the Russian peasants and laborers, they resented the fact that the upper classes had sent them to fight. They demanded equality and democracy. In the turmoil and anger, the ruling elite in Europe lived in fear of more communist revolutions.

In the United States, black soldiers returning from war had a similar experience: After risking their lives for their country, they came home to find that their jobs had been taken, and nobody would hire them because of rampant prejudice. When they demanded their rights, angry whites banded together to terrorize the blacks into submission, killing in cold blood any blacks who dared to demand equal treatment. Riots broke out all over the country, with the largest in Washington, D.C., Chicago, and

Tennessee. Dozens of people were killed, and thousands of black families lost their homes to arson. President Wilson publicly blamed whites for instigating the violence, but—mindful that Southern whites formed a powerful coalition within the Democratic Party—was slow to take action against the perpetrators of violence.

Trial by Fire

*"The test of our progress is not whether we add
more to the abundance of those who have much; it is
whether we provide enough for those who have too little."*
— **Franklin Delano Roosevelt**

resident Wilson suffered a stroke that left him unable
to run for reelection. As the presidential election of
1920 approached, Democrats found themselves in
disarray with no leading candidate. To make matters
worse, a steel strike grabbed the nation's headlines.
More than three hundred and fifty thousand steel workers walked
off the job, and steel production in the United States came to
a grinding halt. The Republicans denounced the strikers—
and the Democrats who supported labor—as dangerous

communists intent on bringing a Russian-type revolution to the United States. Because so many laborers and strikers were immigrants, the Republicans also stoked fears that immigrants were importing dangerous and un-American ideas. The United States, at the time, had an open-door immigration policy. Republicans promised to restrict immigration.

Steel workers threatening to strike listen to a speaker, 1919

At a convention in Chicago in June of 1920, the Republicans nominated Ohio Senator Warren G. Harding for president and Massachusetts Governor Calvin Coolidge for vice president. Both men were archconservatives who advocated repealing all taxes and removing all government regulations from business. Both were opposed to labor unions. Hearing this, Franklin said, "The progressive movement within the Republican Party has been dying since 1916. Yesterday it died."

Three weeks after the Republican convention, Democrats held their convention in San Francisco's Civic Auditorium. Franklin attended as a delegate from New York—and brought a large group of his own supporters. Instead of staying in a hotel, he arranged for accommodations for himself and his supporters aboard a warship docked in the harbor. Though he revealed little about his plans, the size of his retinue suggested that he had ambitions for himself.

The delegates had a difficult time selecting a presidential candidate. They went through forty-four rounds of voting until at last, they settled on Ohio Governor James Cox. Several possible names were put forward for a vice presidential candidate. (At the time, the delegates selected both the presidential and vice presidential candidates.)

Judge Timothy T. Ansberry from Ohio nominated Franklin, saying, "The young man whose name I am going to suggest is but three years over the age of thirty-five prescribed by the

Roosevelt with James Cox, the Democratic ticket in 1920

Constitution . . . but he has crowded into that short period a very large experience as a public figure. His name is a name to conjure with American politics: Franklin D. Roosevelt." The delegates from two more states seconded the motion. When Cox said he preferred Roosevelt, the others withdrew their names. Franklin was selected as the Democratic vice presidential nominee by an acclamation of cheers and shouts.

✳ ✳ ✳ ✳ ✳ ✳ ✳ ✳ ✳ ✳ ✳ ✳ ✳ ✳ ✳

In late September, when the campaign was in full swing, Franklin wrote to Eleanor and asked her to campaign with him. "I miss you so much," he wrote. "It is very strange not to have you with me in all these doings." One historian suggested that Franklin wanted her at his side because it was the first year that women were allowed to vote in presidential elections, and he thought her presence would help appeal to women voters. Eleanor set aside her own work to campaign with him. They traveled the country with a full staff of secretaries, press aides, and advisors, including Louis Howe. It was the most energetic and extensive campaign ever conducted by a candidate for national office. Franklin delivered almost a thousand speeches in three months.

Eleanor was the only woman in the retinue. Initially her job was to signal to Franklin when his speeches went on too long, and to appear gracious while standing next to him. It was Louis Howe who recognized Eleanor's intelligence and political talents. He started approaching her with speeches and asking her opinion. "I was flattered," Eleanor said. "Before long I found myself discussing a range of topics." For the first time, Eleanor felt like an equal partner in her husband's career. She was grateful to Louis.

With public opinion firmly on the side of the Republicans

and against the labor strikers, it soon
became obvious that Cox and
Franklin would lose the election.
Franklin remained cheerful and
optimistic all the way until the
final votes were counted and the
Republicans won one of the most
sweeping victories in presidential
history: Harding won the presidency with about sixteen million

Warren G. Harding, 1920

votes to the Democrats' nine million. Republicans also won control of both the House and the Senate. Republicans, triumphant,
declared that the 1920s would be the decade of business.

S oon to be out of his job as assistant secretary of the navy,
Franklin accepted a position as vice president of the
Fidelity and Deposit Company of Maryland, in charge of the
New York offices. Eleanor plunged back into work of her own.
She was then working on behalf of laborers, particularly women.
She joined the League of Women Voters and further expanded
her circle of female activist friends.

In August of 1921, the family planned a vacation to Sara's home on Campobello Island in New Brunswick, Canada. Anna was then fifteen, James thirteen, Elliott ten, Franklin Jr. seven, and the youngest, John, was five. They were accompanied by their household staff, and Louis Howe—now a close family friend as well as political advisor.

The family plunged into a round of activities: deep-sea fishing in the Bay of Fundy, sailing, tennis, baseball. There were daily picnics, and evening activities by the light of the fireplace.

On August 10, five days after they arrived, they spent the morning sailing, and part of the afternoon helping to put out a small fire on a nearby island. At about four o'clock, Franklin felt shaky. He ignored it and challenged the children to run with him to their favorite swimming place. Later, when they returned to the house, Franklin felt tired, and very odd. "I never quite felt that way before," he said.

The next morning, he woke up with a temperature of 102 degrees Fahrenheit and had trouble moving his left leg. "I tried to persuade myself that the trouble with my leg was muscular, that it would disappear as I used it. But presently it refused to work, and then the other collapsed as well." He was in acute pain and knew something was terribly wrong, but when his daughter, alarmed, asked how he was, he smiled and said he had just a touch of fever.

Eleanor sent for a doctor, Dr. Eben H. Bennet, who diagnosed Franklin with a bad cold. Franklin knew it wasn't a cold. When he didn't improve, Eleanor sent for another doctor, an expert diagnostician, Dr. William W. Keen, who thought he had a blood clot in his lower spinal cord. A few days later, Dr. Keen changed his mind and said Franklin had a spinal lesion. Meanwhile, Franklin was in bed, flat on his back, in severe agony. Eleanor slept on a couch in his room, nursing him day and night. She bathed him, massaged him according to the doctor's instructions, and even brushed his teeth.

Two weeks after Franklin fell ill, a specialist from Boston diagnosed poliomyelitis, also known as infantile paralysis, or more commonly, polio. It was one of the most feared diseases in the early twentieth century. Most often, it struck children, leaving thousands paralyzed each year. When Franklin heard the diagnosis, he was in pain, and running a 100-degree temperature. "He looked very strained and tired," Eleanor said, but when he heard the bad news, "he was completely calm."

In early September, Franklin was moved from Campobello to a New York hospital. He spent six weeks there, with Eleanor in constant attendance. Doctors worried at his "very slow recovery, both as regards the disappearance of pain . . . and as to the recovery of even slight power to twitch the muscles."

The doctors told Franklin that he would probably never walk again, but he wasn't hearing any of it. He insisted he would get better. He was soon firing off cheerful letters to close friends and family, insisting he would soon be walking without crutches. When visitors arrived, they found him all smiles. If someone tried to offer condolences, he brushed it away. His visitors left feeling happier than when they arrived.

"He has such courage, such ambition," observed one of his doctors, "it will take all the skill which we can muster to lead him successfully to a recognition of what he really faces without crushing him." When he was released from the hospital, he began a grueling exercise routine to try to regain strength in his legs. He also worked to build his upper body, arms and chest, hoping to be able to hoist himself in and out of his wheelchair. He hid his pain from everyone, even his closest friends and family, with the same grit that had allowed him as a boy of eight to hide the excruciating pain of a toothache. Except the times when his face was twisted with concentration as he tried to move one of his legs or hoist himself into a wheelchair, he always wore a lighthearted smile.

Initially his children were heartbroken to see him struggling to stand on his own legs, but soon, buoyed by his constant good cheer, they adjusted and assisted in his recovery. Eleanor noted Franklin was helped enormously by the "perfect naturalness with which the children accepted his limitations."

He was fitted with heavy metal braces that ran from his heel to above his waist. The braces locked at the knee to help him stand. After months of practice, he could stand up in the braces, if he had something or someone to lean on. "Walking" meant ratcheting himself forward one halting step at a time, which he could only do if holding on to a person with his left hand and tucking a crutch under his right arm. He wasn't actually walking, though. He was using the strength in his hips to swing his limp legs forward.

Sara believed it was time for Franklin to give up politics and retire to the ease of Hyde Park. Indeed, in the 1920s, it was unheard of for those who were disabled—then called "cripples"—to work professionally.

Eleanor, on the other hand, understood that Franklin would never be fulfilled or happy living quietly at Hyde Park. She also understood that to remain active in politics, he needed her help. She rose to the occasion. While he spent his days working with medical professionals to try to regain some control of his legs, she attended political meetings and gave speeches in his name, making sure the Democratic Party would not forget their 1920 vice presidential nominee.

Franklin said he would not reenter politics until he'd made as full a recovery as possible—a decision that seemed entirely practical, but also happened to be politically savvy. The political landscape during the 1920s was not good for Democrats. The Republicans had deregulated businesses and banks, and as a result, business and industry were booming. Banks were freely lending money. Consumers who could afford them were buying modern goods like refrigerators and radios. Henry Ford's

By this time, the Republican Party had adopted a policy known as laissez-faire economics or free market economy, a theory of economics that holds that the economy works best when the government stays out of the way and refrains from interfering. Those who adopted this idea were opposed to such governmental regulations as minimum wages for workers, maximum work hours, or mandating safe workplaces. The theory was that the market would take assembly-line-produced Model T Ford allowed more Americans to afford cars. Factories were churning out products.

The decade of the 1920s was, on the surface, a time of prosperity for America. It was the Jazz Age and a time of high spirits. Women defied centuries of tradition by shortening their skirts and cutting their hair. People felt they were still celebrating the end of the Great War.

Not everyone prospered, however. Beneath the glittering surface there were rumblings of discontent. Because factory and business owners had complete freedom in how they ran their factories, wages remained low even as businesses grew more profitable. As a result, the gap between laborers and business

care of itself based on supply and demand. Free market proponents said that personal liberty meant that if a worker agreed to work ten hours in exchange for a few pennies, it was none of the government's business. Those who embraced laissez-faire economics argued that if employers offered bad working conditions, people would look for other jobs. They also believed that taxing businesses penalized them for high levels of production.

Fashion for women before the 1920s reflected the times, featuring restrictive clothing that forced the body into unnatural shapes. But with prosperity came a freer spirit, a more relaxed lifestyle, at least for those who could afford it. *Left*: Images from 1911 dress patterns. *Right*: Dress patterns from the 1920s "flapper" style.

executives widened as millions of laborers worked long days for poverty-level wages while the business tycoons grew wealthier.

Only the very rich—about 5 percent of the population—could afford to send their children to college. In fact, money was just about all a person needed to gain admission to the nation's best universities, which created a cycle: Because only the wealthy could afford college, only the wealthy were qualified for high-level jobs. Laborers working ten or twelve hours each day to feed their families had no choice but to put their own children to work as soon as they were old enough, thus setting them up for a lifetime of low-skill and low-wage labor. Immigrants were discriminated against and thus had more difficulty lifting themselves from poverty. Blacks, segregated with fewer opportunities than whites, had it hardest of all.

✶ ✶ ✶ ✶ ✶ ✶ ✶ ✶ ✶ ✶ ✶ ✶ ✶ ✶

The 1924 Democratic Convention was planned for late June at Madison Square Garden in New York City. The primary task of the convention was to select the Democratic nominees for president and vice president. The contest for nomination for president was between New York Governor Al Smith, and Representative John Davis of West Virginia. Al Smith asked Franklin to put his name into nomination, which meant going onto the stage and addressing the delegates. Franklin accepted. It would be his first public appearance since being stricken with polio.

Franklin was determined to surprise everyone by walking on the stage, which would require braces, a crutch, and the arm of his sixteen-year-old son, James. He practiced for weeks to prepare for the moment.

Franklin on crutches on the porch of the Roosevelt home in Hyde Park. He's with George Lunn, John W. Davis, and Alfred E. Smith (*left to right*).

On the morning the convention opened, he was driven to a side entrance and then lifted into his wheelchair. James wheeled him inside. He and James waited backstage. When their cue came, James locked Franklin's braces and pulled him to a standing position so he could enter the convention on his feet. Grasping his son's upper arm with his left hand, and leaning on a crutch tucked under his right arm, Franklin thrust himself forward one tiny step at a time in a slow, halting rhythm. The audience watched in complete silence as he inched himself to the podium while standing upright.

When he reached the podium, he turned to face the audience, drew himself up to full height, and smiled. The hall exploded with cheers. He then gave what was later said to be the most memorable speech of the convention. After extolling Smith's virtues and explaining why he was the right candidate to lead the Democratic Party, Franklin said:

> *He has a personality that carries to every hearer not*
> *only the sincerity but the righteousness of what he says.*
> *He is the "Happy Warrior" of the political battlefield . . .*
> *Alfred E. Smith.*

When he finished his speech, the cheers were ear-splitting. The pandemonium lasted more than an hour. "The crowd just went crazy," said one observer. "It was stupendous, really stupendous." The crowd burst into song. People swayed and yelled themselves hoarse. Franklin's eternal optimism and jaunty high spirits took on a new meaning: He was now viewed as a man oblivious to personal suffering, a man who hid a core of strength behind a cheerful face.

The band played "The Sidewalks of New York," and the crowd continued cheering as James returned his father to his chair, helped to ease him into a sitting position, and wheeled him offstage. The *New York Herald Tribune* reported from the convention that Franklin was easily the foremost figure on the floor or platform. His speech nominating Smith was remembered as his "Happy Warrior Speech"—but it was Franklin who was remembered as the happy warrior.

Al Smith didn't get the nomination, but Franklin's speech saved him from crushing defeat. The nomination went to John Davis of West Virginia. As Franklin suspected, the Democrats didn't stand a chance against the Republicans that year. With the Decade of Business—also called the Decade of Optimism—in full swing, Republican candidate Calvin Coolidge glided easily to victory with over twenty-one million votes to Smith's fifteen million. Coolidge swept every state except twelve in the South that were still unwilling to vote for the party of Lincoln.

✴ ✴ ✴ ✴ ✴ ✴ ✴ ✴ ✴ ✴ ✴ ✴ ✴

Franklin tried one cure after another, none of which worked. Meanwhile, he kept up an exercise and physical therapy regimen. He also worked hard at politics, writing letters, congratulating Democrats who won races, consoling those who did not, asking and giving advice, inviting guests to visit him.

Being a happy warrior got a little easier in 1924, when he learned about the warm, soothing mineral waters of Warm

Springs, Georgia. The minerals in the water—bicarbonate, silica, calcium, magnesium, sulfate, and potassium—lifted people up so they felt as if they were standing, or walking in the water, a glorious and liberating feeling to someone confined to a wheelchair.

Franklin had a new personal secretary, the extraordinarily competent and devoted Marguerite LeHand, nicknamed "Missy" because one of Franklin's sons had trouble saying "Miss LeHand." In October, Franklin, Eleanor, and a group that included Missy, journeyed to Georgia to try the springs. Franklin and the others arrived at a depot with two entrances, one marked WHITE and one marked COLORED. The town itself was "not much beyond the horse-and-buggy stage . . . The little whitewashed cottages were dilapidated, and the single hotel in town was pretty run-down."

The soothing waters worked: The warmth not only eased Franklin's pain, but the minerals enabled him to walk in the water. The experience infused him with a new hope that one day he'd be able to walk without the help of the mineral water. He fell in love with everything about the springs, including the town itself. He enjoyed meeting the local townspeople and immediately made friends with them.

Eleanor, in contrast, disliked everything about central

Georgia. She didn't like the harsh segregation. She didn't like the fact that black people lived in deplorable conditions. She began asking questions, and didn't bother to hide her disapproval of how the local whites treated the blacks. The feeling was mutual. Later, when Eleanor became known as an anti-segregation activist, a local "white Southern lady" said, "We didn't like her a bit. She ruined every maid we ever had."

It didn't take Eleanor long to find an excuse to return to New York. She was then editing the *Women's Democratic News*, a political newsletter, and she was an active member of the Women's Trade Union League, so she had engagements to attend.

★ ★ ★ ★ ★ ★ ★ ★ ★ ★ ★ ★ ★

I can still remember the day [Franklin] almost made it," said a friend visiting Warm Springs. Franklin, determined to walk across the room without help, "braced himself against one wall in the living room, and the nurse walked backward in front of him. Slowly, ever so slowly, he forced his body across the room—one inch at a time, it seemed. He was so drenched in sweat I was afraid he would collapse from exhaustion." Missy, watching, was in tears.

At the end of the ordeal, the friend saw what he believed

was the anguish of realization in Franklin's eyes. That was the moment—his friend believed—when Franklin truly understood he would never walk again. For the remainder of Franklin's life, though, he insisted one day he'd walk again with ease. Six years after his illness, he wrote to his doctor, "My own legs continue to improve," but "I cannot get rid of the brace on that left leg yet. It is still a mystery to me as to why that left knee declines to lock . . . "

Franklin invested two-thirds of his entire personal fortune to restore the Warm Springs hotel and spa. He purchased the grounds, all the cottages, and the pools. He formed the Warm Springs Foundation with a panel of distinguished backers. The foundation offered free use of the facilities to anyone sick and in need of the soothing baths. He had several cottages furnished for his own use and the use of his friends and visitors.

Before long, he was the spirited center of a group of men, women, and children struggling to recover use of their limbs or soothe their pain in the waters. He insisted on a lighthearted celebratory mood at all times. He cheered the others on, encouraging them to work toward full recovery. He appointed himself vice president in charge of picnics, and organized outings. Local residents loved him. As always, there was serious purpose under his jovial manners. He talked politics with local leaders, including the judge and sheriff. He spoke in local Sunday schools. His political contacts in Georgia became important later.

For the rest of his life, he made regular trips to Warm Springs, for the soothing warm waters, the camaraderie—and for the exhilarating feeling that he was walking once more.

Franklin in the waters of Warm Springs, Georgia, 1929

The Great Depression

*"Take a method and try it.
If it fails admit it frankly and try another.
But above all, try something."*

— Franklin Delano Roosevelt

The Democrats in New York needed a candidate for governor, and they needed one quickly. It was early autumn, 1928, and New York Governor Al Smith had just been nominated once more for president. His opponent was Republican Herbert Hoover. The election would be held in the following year. The problem was that Smith's two-year term as governor was ending in a few months, and he couldn't run for both governor and president. To keep the governorship in Democratic control, the Democrats needed

Al Smith campaigning in 1928

a candidate for New York governor who was well-known and electable.

Franklin chose that moment to tell reporters that he believed he was close to being able to walk again. The public outpouring of well wishes was touching and genuine. This gave the New York Democrats the idea that Franklin was the solution. They remembered his stunning performance at the previous convention. He had a famous name that would draw voters to the polls. But when New York Democratic Party leaders tried to reach him, he avoided their calls. He went on long picnics. He took extended baths in the springs.

The Democratic Party leaders became frantic. Al Smith personally called Eleanor and begged her to contact her husband and persuade him to accept the nomination. When one of the New York Democrats got Franklin on the phone, Franklin turned down the offer several times before coyly accepting.

Shortly after he was nominated, he remarked to an associate that "When you're in politics, you have to play the game." He

Calvin Coolidge and Herbert Hoover, 1928

didn't explain what he meant—but he was now running for New York governor, the very job that years earlier he'd said would be his final step to the White House. And he was able to say the party had begged him to accept the nomination.

New York Republicans, taken aback to learn that Franklin was the Democratic nominee, went on the attack. The *New York Post* declared there was "something pathetic and pitiless in the 'drafting' of Franklin D. Roosevelt." The *Post* said that his nomination was unfair to Franklin, and to the people of New York. Al

Smith had his answer ready. "A governor doesn't have to be an acrobat," he said. "The work of the governorship is brainwork."

Franklin went to New York and energetically barnstormed the state, sometimes making as many as fourteen speeches each day. He and his aides found ways to hide his disability. Two muscular men provided support when he tried to walk. To carry him upstairs, each man grasped one of his elbows and lifted him up the steps in a standing position. To viewers from a distance, Franklin appeared to be walking up the stairs himself. The men lifted him from cars so easily onlookers hardly noticed he was being carried.

He peppered his speeches with jokes. Most people run for governor, he said, but "I am counting on my friends all over the state to make it possible for me to walk in." He impressed onlookers with his physical stamina. Initially people assumed he'd lose. His Republican opponent, Albert Ottinger—New York attorney general, and former assistant attorney general of the United States—was a well-respected prosecutor and a strong candidate, but the outpouring of enthusiasm for Franklin took everyone by surprise. Franklin ended his campaign in Poughkeepsie, where twenty thousand people paraded down Main Street in his honor.

On election day, Franklin voted in Hyde Park, and then went to his campaign headquarters at the Biltmore Hotel in New York

City to listen to the returns. By about nine in the evening, it was clear the Republicans would have another nationwide landslide. Hoover even won some of the South, winning Virginia, North Carolina, Florida, Tennessee, and Texas.

The New York governor's race, however, was so close that at midnight it wasn't clear who would win. Franklin was running slightly behind Ottinger. He announced that he was going home to get some sleep. Louis Howe and a team of advisors and supporters stayed to keep track of the returns. Among those who remained was Sara, who said, "It's not over by a long shot." She didn't want her son to stay in politics, but if he did, she intended to be his strongest supporter.

At 2:00 a.m. Franklin caught up. By 4:00 a.m. he had pulled far enough ahead so that it was clear he would squeak out a win. Sara joined the men in a toast, and then she and another woman who'd stayed took a taxi to wake Franklin up and tell him the good news.

✴ ✴ ✴ ✴ ✴ ✴ ✴ ✴ ✴ ✴ ✴ ✴ ✴ ✴ ✴

The Roosevelts moved into the Governor's Mansion. Franklin's oldest child, Anna, now twenty-two, had married a stockbroker and was living in Manhattan. James was in his final year at Harvard, and the younger boys were at Groton, under the care of Endicott Peabody, Franklin's former headmaster.

Louis and Franklin's secretary, Missy, also moved in. There was a constant stream of visitors: newspaper reporters, friends, politicians, distinguished guests. The Roosevelt boys were in and out of the mansion when visiting from school, often bringing friends with them. Meals were boisterous affairs, with everyone eating together and multiple conversations happening at once. All nine of the guest bedrooms were usually occupied.

An elevator was installed at the mansion to accommodate Franklin's wheelchair. The greenhouse was removed, and a swimming pool built in its place. Franklin loved movies, but because most public places were not equipped to accommodate wheelchairs, he had difficulty attending theaters, so a screen was set up on the third floor.

In the evenings, Roosevelt enjoyed relaxing with friends and making small talk. At least once each week, everyone gathered in the screening room to watch a new release. Eleanor, who was uncomfortable with lighthearted banter, often worked in the evenings. She was even known to work until 11:50 p.m. on New Year's Eve, join the party for a few minutes to cheer in the New Year, and then return to work.

Eleanor acted as a surrogate governor, often attending events and speaking for Franklin when mobility issues made travel too difficult. She felt challenged and involved, and enjoyed her new role. Their daughter, Anna, later said that "The polio was very instrumental in bringing them much closer in a very real partnership."

Franklin appointed women to official positions, saying, "It is my firm belief that had women had an equal share in making laws in years past, the unspeakable conditions in crowded tenements, the neglect of the poor, the unwillingness to spend money for hospitals would never have come about." Farms had been in a state of decline in New York for years, partly because of the high price of water and utilities, which, at the time, were owned and controlled by private interests and businesses. Franklin wanted the state government to build and operate its own dams and utility companies to keep costs to consumers down.

He ran into strong resistance: The companies that profited from selling water and electricity denounced what they called tyrannical government control. They fought so hard against his attempts to regulate utilities and waterworks that he wasn't able to make much progress.

Another hardship for farmers was that they had been forced

to pay to maintain their own roads and highways and to contribute to the cost of public education. In April of 1929, Franklin signed legislation requiring the State of New York to assume more of the costs of roads and local education, reducing the financial burden on farmers.

That same month, Franklin began his signature radio programs—later called Fireside Chats—in which he talked directly to New Yorkers. Radio had been invented a few decades earlier, but the new technology had only recently become widely available. Franklin's talks gave listeners the impression he was ensconced in an armchair. "You felt he was talking to you, not 50 million others but to you personally," said one contemporary. In fact, Franklin went through many drafts of each talk before delivering it, editing, breaking down complex policies and decisions so they could be easily grasped and understood. His main goal was to reach the voters in upstate New York, who got their news mostly from Republican newspapers. As a result of his radio programs, his popularity soared.

✶ ✶ ✶ ✶ ✶ ✶ ✶ ✶ ✶ ✶ ✶ ✶ ✶ ✶ ✶

n October 29, 1929, a day later known as Black Tuesday, the Decade of Business came to a screeching halt. The stock market crashed, losing billions of dollars in a single day, wiping out the entire savings of millions of Americans, and bankrupting businesses and factories.

The stock market, or a stock exchange, is a place where stocks are bought and sold. Businesses raise money by selling stocks—or shares of the business—which allows individuals to invest in companies. If a business does well, the value of the company increases. Stock prices rise, and the investors earn money. If a business does poorly, the value of the company decreases. Stock prices drop, and the investors lose money.

A stock market crash happens when stock prices plummet, and people who invested in stocks lose their money.

Economists now agree that the stock market crash of 1929, like previous economic panics, had multiple causes. One of the causes is what economists call a bubble created by artificially high stock prices. While businesses had been booming and stock prices were high, everyone wanted to buy stock. Those without

Thousands of people gather outside the New York Stock Exchange following the crash of 1929.

cash were allowed to buy "on margin," meaning they paid only a small amount and borrowed the rest from a bank or stockbroker.

The demand for stocks pushed the prices higher and higher, but the values of the companies selling the stocks didn't rise. When people realized they had borrowed large amounts of money to buy stocks that were worth a fraction of what they had paid, they quickly sold, causing the prices to plummet. Plummeting prices created a downward spiral because people saw the falling prices, panicked, and sold more of their stock, causing the prices to drop further.

Another related cause of the stock market crash was that business owners and tycoons had been manipulating the market so they could profit. For example, several well-respected investors, or speculators, would agree to suddenly buy lots of a particular company's stock. Others would see what they were doing and assumed the stock was valuable, so they, too, would buy, pushing the price higher and higher. Once the price was artificially high, the speculators would sell their stock at a large profit. Thus consumers were tricked into borrowing money to buy stocks

When banks began closing, people panicked and rushed to banks and demanded their deposits back, 1933.

at artificially inflated prices. Those who favored laissez-faire economics argued that all was fair under a concept called caveat emptor (buyer beware). The idea behind caveat emptor was that if people were duped, it was their own fault for not being wiser.

The meaning and limits of personal liberty have been debated since the founding of the nation.

Those who favor laissez-faire economics believe that personal liberty is achieved when government regulations are minimal. They argue that fewer regulations enables business to prosper, which helps everyone.

Those opposed to laissez-faire economics believe personal liberty does not include the freedom to behave in a manner that tramples the rights of others. They argue that liberty must be curtailed when exercising it tramples the rights of others. Roosevelt, for example, believed that government can curtail the excesses of capitalism that allow for cheating and taking advantage of others.

When the stock market crashed on Black Tuesday, "people felt that the ground under their feet was giving way." With so many businesses suddenly bankrupt and people wiped out of their savings, many consumers stopped spending money for goods, particularly luxury goods, which caused the prices of goods to plummet, creating another downward spiral. Factories, unable to sell their goods, failed and closed. Factories closing caused large numbers of people to lose their jobs, which threw families into crisis.

As businesses across the nation closed their doors, banks also began to fail because they had loaned large amounts of money to businesses, which were now unable to repay the loans. People were terrified that they were going to lose their savings, so they rushed to withdraw their money from banks. This, in turn, caused more banks to fail. The economic crisis—called the Great Depression—spread to Europe partially because nations like Germany depended on credit from American banks to help them recover from the war.

President Hoover, a proponent of laissez-faire economics, believed government interference would make the problem worse. He recognized, however, that the crisis was deepening because of the general panic. Until public faith could be restored, people would hoard their cash instead of spending or depositing it in a bank. Without money circulating, the economy would continue to slump.

Hoover asked industry leaders to meet and find ways to keep their factories open and avoid cutting wages to restore public faith in the dollar. Unfortunately, business leaders were unable to come to a consensus on the best way to deal with the problem— so they accomplished nothing.

A New Deal

*"We have always known that heedless self interest was
bad morals, we now know that it is bad economics."*
— *Franklin Delano Roosevelt*

Franklin was among the first elected leaders to conclude
that the economic crisis would not right itself out. He
searched for solutions. First, he pushed for New York
government-sponsored programs to help state residents
who were suddenly unemployed and needed money to
buy food. Then he set up an emergency employment committee
to formulate a plan for stabilizing unemployment.

He was in his first term when the Great Depression hit. He
campaigned for reelection on the need to help the state's farmers.

"If the farmer starves today," Franklin said to an audience in December, "we all starve tomorrow." He also campaigned on the high costs of water and electricity, promising to continue fighting the big corporations that were keeping prices inflated. He made the point about the cost of electricity so strongly, using the example of a new invention, the electric waffle iron, that his campaign came to be known as the Waffle Iron Campaign.

He campaigned against laissez-faire economics, which he argued put too much power into the hands of banks and business owners. At the annual Jefferson Day dinner of the National Democratic Club in New York City, he invoked the spirit of Jefferson, who had distrusted banks and industrialists, by saying, "If Thomas Jefferson were alive he would be the first to question this concentration of economic power."

His Republican opponent wanted the election to be about corruption in the New York Democratic Party. Franklin ignored him and talked about the incompetence of Republican President Hoover's administration. He explained his strategy to a friend: "Never let your opponent pick the battleground on which to fight. If he picks one, stay out of it and let him fight all by himself."

This time, he coasted to victory, winning forty-one of the

fifty-seven counties outside of New York City. It was a personal triumph and an unprecedented victory for a Democrat in New York.

The day after the election, Howe and another of Franklin's advisors, James Farley, held a press conference and hinted that Franklin would run for president in 1932. "I do not see how Mr. Roosevelt can escape becoming the next presidential nominee of his party," Farley told the members of the press, "even if no one should raise a finger to bring it about."

Democratic hopes to retake the White House were soaring: Republicans, in the 1920s, had assured the nation that as long as Republicans were elected, the economy was safe. Now there were soup kitchens, and homeless shelters called Hoovervilles, scornfully named after the president. The Republicans had taken credit for the economic boom. Now they were blamed for the crash.

Franklin kicked off his second term as New York governor by recommending a New York pension law to provide for elderly people who had worked all their lives, but because of low wages, had been unable to save enough for their old age. Next he set about trying to persuade the state legislature to establish a state-funded Temporary Emergency Relief Administration, the

TERA. People lucky enough to have a job were often required to work more than twelve-hour days, six days per week, at starvation wages to keep their jobs. Franklin passed a bill limiting women and children to a six-day, forty-eight-hour workweek. He tried to introduce a minimum wage for all workers, but was met with a powerful resistance from the business and factory owners, who claimed that the higher costs would drive factories to other states.

With an eye on the next presidential election, Franklin assembled a diverse group of advisors, including university professors and the nation's top economists, which he called his brain trust. To counter fears that his paralysis would render him unable to undertake the duties of the presidency, he asked a select panel of top doctors, including a brain specialist, to examine him and write a report on his health. They did, and reported that his "health and powers of endurance are such as to allow him to meet any demand of private and public life." Indeed, his exercise routine had so built his upper body that he could swing himself in and out of chairs, and up and down stairs using railings like gymnastics bars.

Depression-era breadlines. Original caption read: "Hunger line, Sixth Ave and 42nd Street, NYC." February 1932.

✦ ✦ ✦ ✦ ✦ ✦ ✦ ✦ ✦ ✦ ✦ ✦ ✦ ✦

The Democratic Convention was held in Chicago, Illinois, beginning June 27, 1932. Franklin was the leading candidate for the Democratic presidential nomination, but because of a rule requiring the winner to earn two-thirds of the delegate votes, his nomination was not certain. His chief rival was the very man he had called the happy warrior, Al Smith, who had preceded him as New York's governor. Franklin's advisors and strategists, led by Howe, devised a national campaign, mobilizing supporters throughout the country. By the time of the convention, Franklin had a majority of delegates pledged to him.

As was common at the time, Franklin didn't attend the convention. He, his family, Missy, Howe, and a few others gathered in the sitting room in the Governor's Mansion in Albany and listened as the convention was broadcast on the radio. When, after multiple rounds of voting, it was clear Franklin would win the nomination, he sent a telegram to Thomas J. Walsh of Montana, chair of the convention, saying that he planned to travel by plane to Chicago and accept the nomination in person.

Walsh read Roosevelt's telegram from the stage. The entire convention—and soon the entire nation—buzzed with excitement. Air travel was not easy in those days, and no presidential candidate had ever before traveled by plane.

✶ ✶ ✶ ✶ ✶ ✶ ✶ ✶ ✶ ✶ ✶ ✶ ✶ ✶ ✶

Franklin boarded a plane in New York with Eleanor, sons Elliott and John, Missy, and several advisors. He was fully aware of the symbolism of his flight. He would be president of a modern America. His disability would not prevent him from traveling at the spur of the moment. The flight from New York to Chicago took nine hours and ran into dangerous winds. The plane had to land twice to refuel, once in Buffalo and once in Cleveland.

Hordes of supporters were waiting for them at the airport in Chicago. They all traveled from the airport to the convention in a triumphant procession. When Franklin took the stage to accept the nomination, there was a thunderous applause. The band played "Happy Days Are Here Again," a song that came to be associated with him.

Franklin told the audience that he was campaigning on a promise to bring America a party of "liberal thought, of planned action, of enlightened international outlook, and of the greatest good to the greatest number of our citizens." Nestled in the speech were the words that would one day become the most famous: "new deal." What he said was: "I pledge you, I pledge myself, to a new deal for the American People."

★　★　★　★　★　★　★　★　★　★　★　★　★　★

Franklin campaigned as he always did: with impressive energy, charm, wit, and buoyancy.

He spoke about the economy in shambles. He accused the Republicans of refusing to do anything about it. "Must the country remain hungry and jobless while raw materials stand unused and factories idle?" he asked during a campaign event in Georgia. "The country needs, the country demands, bold, persistent experimentation."

Franklin spoke familiarly to audiences, calling everyone by their first names, but by this time only his family and closest friends, including Louis Howe, called him Franklin. To everyone else, he was Mr. Roosevelt. At the age of forty-four, despite his outward joviality, he had developed an "unspoken dignity, an impenetrable reserve that protected him against undue familiarity."

His friends described him as complicated. His enemies said he was devious. Those closest to him understood he was elusive, hiding his thoughts and motives behind a face that had two

Tenant farmers, now homeless, Oklahoma, 1936

expressions: happy or serene. Eleanor explained his personality by saying that because he "disliked being disagreeable, he made an effort to give each person who came in contact with him the feeling that he understood what his particular interest was." She also said that because he often nodded his head and frequently said, "I see," or something of that sort, people often thought he was in full agreement with what they were saying. In fact, he was taking in all opinions, processing them, and formulating his own ideas.

Roosevelt's paralysis had an unexpected effect on voters. Instead of being concerned that he would be unable to perform the duties of office, many who watched as he "walked" with the help of companions, or swung himself down stairs using the banisters, often felt a rush of respect for the man who had conquered his disability by sheer willpower and determination. One broadcaster concluded that anyone with such patience and determination had the qualities to lead a devastated nation to recovery.

When a journalist asked Eleanor if she thought her husband could stand the strain of being president, she said, "If the infantile paralysis didn't kill him, the Presidency won't."

As the good news poured in on election night, Roosevelt celebrated with his friends, family, and supporters at his campaign headquarters in New York City. The Democrats picked up ninety-seven seats in the House of Representatives, and won solid majorities in both houses of Congress. The turnout was impressive: Nearly forty million Americans voted in the 1932 election. Roosevelt won the presidency, carrying forty-two states, receiving almost twenty-three million votes to Hoover's sixteen million.

Action, and Action Now

The four months between Roosevelt's election and his inauguration were among the most harrowing in American memory. It was the fourth winter of the Depression. Five thousand banks across the nation had closed. Fifteen million workers, one-fourth of the entire labor force, were unemployed. Many who still had jobs had taken such drastic cuts in wages they were not earning enough to buy food for their families. One scholar estimated that one-quarter of the entire population didn't have enough money for adequate food.

Gross farm income was reduced by half. Homeowners were losing their homes and schools had no money to pay teachers. Malnutrition and starvation was widespread, particularly in the poorer, rural states like West Virginia and Kentucky.

The economic crisis increased the confusion in Europe, where various parties were vying for control of the newly created countries. In some places, democracy was having trouble taking hold. Some people felt frustrated by the inefficiency of the new governments. Democracy, by its very nature, is slow-working. Representative government requires give-and-take and compromise. A monarch or emperor, in contrast, doesn't have to do much compromising, and there are fewer checks and balances hindering him.

In the new democratic government of Germany put in place after World War I, Jews and other minorities enjoyed rights equal to ethnic Germans. Freedom brought other changes as well. The Jazz Age came to Berlin. Night clubs and cabarets sprang up. There was an openly gay community in Berlin—which many people found shocking and upsetting. Such rapid changes alarmed certain segments of the German population.

From the chaos, a new movement arose called fascism.

Fascists held a view directly opposite to Roosevelt's. While Roosevelt believed the purpose of government was to regulate industry and private interests and to better the life of the citizens, fascists believe the purpose of government is to protect people from enemies, which can be best accomplished by a small group controlling both the government and the nation's industries.

Fascists are backwards looking. They pine for a time in the past when the nation had mythic greatness. The fascist leader tells the people their suffering is the fault of their enemies. The "enemies" are generally racial, religious, or immigrant groups who, according to the fascist leader, threaten the "purity" of the nation.

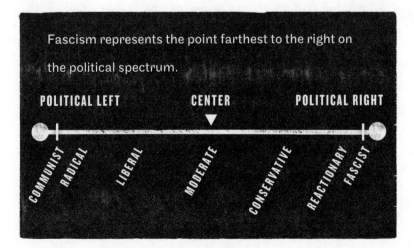

Fascism represents the point farthest to the right on the political spectrum.

POLITICAL LEFT   CENTER   POLITICAL RIGHT

COMMUNIST RADICAL LIBERAL MODERATE CONSERVATIVE REACTIONARY FASCIST

Some scholars believe fascism is caused by external conditions, like economic depression. Others, like scholars Karen Stenner and Jonathan Haidt, argue that such uprisings are a predictable feature of democracies. Liberals tend to push democracies toward greater diversity by expanding voting rights and inclusiveness. Stenner and Haidt describe what they call a right-wing authoritarian personality. People with this personality have a natural aversion to complexity, which includes diversity. They favor sameness, conformity, and obedience. Stenner and others conclude that across

Adolph Hitler's rise to power was typical of a fascist: He gave fiery speeches telling the German people—who were still suffering economically from World War I—that they had been betrayed by Jewish people living in their midst. Jews, a minority group, had long faced discrimination in Europe. Hitler told the Germans that the Depression had been caused by evil bankers, and that the banking industry was controlled by Jews, who were creating problems for everyone from their own greed. He promised to restore Germany to greatness.

Western liberal democracies, about a third of the population is inclined toward authoritarianism.

They also describe an "authoritarian dynamic" that happens like this: The growing diversity that occurs naturally in a liberal democracy ignites anger in right-wing authoritarians, who want to return to a more orderly past. When their fears are aroused—usually by a leader who deliberately stokes their angers and fears—they are capable of cruelty. Thus, a cycle emerges: As liberalism expands, right-wing authoritarians react. According to this theory, Hitler rose to power on a backlash against Europe's growing diversity.

Germany held elections in November of 1932, the same month Roosevelt was elected president. Hitler's Nazi Party captured only 33 percent of the vote, and thus failed to

Adolph Hitler. On his armband is the Nazi symbol, the swastika. Forms of the swastika have ancient roots, but the Nazis adapted it to symbolize what they called German nationalistic pride. The Nazi flag featured the swastika placed in a circle.

win control of Parliament by two million votes. Hitler came to power, though, through a backroom deal. An influential German named Franz von Papen, who wanted the position of vice chancellor, entered a coalition with the Nazis. Believing he could contain Hitler, Franz von Papen persuaded his own supporters and numerous influential politicians to back Hitler's appointment as chancellor of Germany. As a result, Hitler was appointed chancellor of Germany on January 30, 1933, with Franz von Papen as vice chancellor.

Hitler insisted he needed emergency war powers so that he could solve Germany's problems—powers that would allow him to act without consent of Parliament and without constitutional constraints. Hitler so effectively badgered government officials that he got his way. Because democratic institutions in Germany were new and not deeply rooted, Hitler was able to bully and crush his political opponents. He outlawed all political parties except the Nazis, and put an end to labor unions. By the time Franz van Papen discovered he could not control Hitler, it was too late: Hitler had taken control of the entire German government, removing all checks and balances against his power.

Hitler was not Europe's first fascist leader. Benito Mussolini created the Fascist Party in Italy in 1919, and was elected prime minister of Italy in 1922. Once he was elected, he seized absolute power, took control of the nation's industries, and ruled as a dictator.

Trouble was brewing in Asia as well. Japanese anger at the West began in the early 1930s when European nations placed barriers on trade with Japan to protect their colonial markets in Asia. Japan, too, had been hit by America's Great Depression and struggled to recover. Because they couldn't look to the West for economic partnerships, Japan's military leaders concluded that the only way to solve Japan's economic difficulties was to expand their borders by conquering neighboring nations. Japanese Prime Minister Inukai Tsuyoshi attempted to rein in the military, but in 1932, he was assassinated by right-wing extremists. Military officers took over the government of Japan, wresting power from the emperor.

Roosevelt watched all of this with alarm. His most pressing task, though, was to lift America from the Great Depression and

Japanese Prime Minister Inukai Tsuyoshi, who tried but failed to control the Japanese armed forces, 1932

select his cabinet members. He appointed a diverse group to his cabinet representing multiple viewpoints, including a few conservative Republicans. He hoped to create a "cooperative commonwealth," in which business, labor, and government could work together to stabilize the economy. He also appointed America's first female cabinet member, Frances Perkins, as secretary of labor. Perkins was a 1902 graduate of Mount Holyoke College. She had gone on to earn her master's degree in sociology and economics from Columbia University. She spent her career investigating labor conditions and lobbying for laws to protect women laborers.

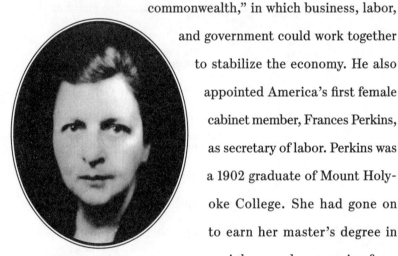

Secretary of Labor Frances Perkins, 1932

Howe would be his chief of staff. Missy, with a staff of her own, would oversee all of the White House secretarial duties.

★ ★ ★ ★ ★ ★ ★ ★ ★ ★ ★ ★ ★ ★ ★

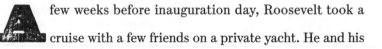 few weeks before inauguration day, Roosevelt took a cruise with a few friends on a private yacht. He and his

traveling companions disembarked at Miami, where he gave a short speech at the annual meeting of the American Legion at Bay Front Park. About twenty thousand legionnaires crammed into the park. He spoke to the crowd perched on the back seat of an open car. When he finished, he slid back into the seat and chatted with the mayor of Chicago, Anton Cermak, who was standing nearby.

Suddenly there was a burst of gunfire followed by a man shouting, "Too many people are starving to death!" The gunman fired toward Roosevelt. He missed the president-elect, but hit and wounded Cermak and several bystanders. The crowd descended into pandemonium—but Roosevelt sat utterly still, unflinching and controlled. Those who saw him were shocked by his calm. The assassin was ready to fire again but his aim was thrown off when an alert bystander hit him with her purse. Secret Service men then wrestled his gun from him.

Roosevelt accompanied Cermak and the others to the hospital. All the victims recovered except Cermak, who died a few weeks later.

The assassin turned out to be an unemployed bricklayer named Giuseppe "Joe" Zangara who was motivated by hatred of wealthy and powerful people. He was tried for murder, and found guilty.

✦ ✦ ✦ ✦ ✦ ✦ ✦ ✦ ✦ ✦ ✦ ✦ ✦ ✦ ✦

Roosevelt's Inauguration Day dawned gray and bleak. According to tradition, the president-elect and the out-going president rode in an open car to the inauguration. Onlookers found the contrast between the two men startling. Herbert Hoover was sour and sullen. Roosevelt was beaming, his head thrust high, offering the crowd his cheerful smile.

Among those Roosevelt had personally invited to his inauguration were thirteen children on crutches whom he knew from Warm Springs. Chief Justice Hughes administered the oath of office on a platform in front of the Capitol rotunda strung with ivy and hung with flags. After Roosevelt repeated the oath, he turned to face the crowd. The wind was cold, rustling the pages of his speech.

"This is a day of national consecration," he began. He went on to assure the American people that the "great nation will endure as it has endured and will revive and will prosper." He paused for emphasis before uttering what would become the most famous words of his speech: "So, first of all, let me assert my firm belief that the only thing we have to fear is fear itself—nameless, unreasoning, unjustified terror which paralyzes . . . " He promised "Action, and action now."

Roosevelt's first inauguration, 1933

✴ ✴ ✴ ✴ ✴ ✴ ✴ ✴ ✴ ✴ ✴ ✴ ✴ ✴

Roosevelt lived up to his promise of immediate action. His first item of business was the banking crisis. The day after his inauguration, he declared a national bank holiday—all banks were to close beginning March 6. With all the banks closed, he drafted the Emergency Banking Relief Act, which put the nation's banks under federal control, and promised them federal aid. Three days later, Congress met in a special session to consider the bill. Both houses passed it and Roosevelt signed it the same day. Encouraged by the promise of government assistance, the strongest banks reopened right away. Three-quarters of the nation's bank reopened by the end of the month.

On March 12, Roosevelt delivered the first of his presidential Fireside Chats. "I just want to talk for a few minutes with the people of the United States about banking," he began. He explained how banks work—money deposited in accounts doesn't sit in vaults. The bank puts the money to work, investing it and lending money in the form of mortgages and credit to keep "the wheels of industry and agriculture turning around." He explained the banking bill, and asked Americans to put their money back into banks, assuring them that "it is safer to keep your money in a reopened bank than it is to keep it under your mattress."

The first Fireside Chat was a resounding success. Millions of Americans redeposited whatever cash funds they had on hand into banks, thereby breathing new life into the nation's financial institutions, which were now able to offer credit to struggling farms and businesses.

With banks reopening and money once more flowing, there was an outpouring of adoration for the new president. Ten thousand telegrams swept the White House in a single week. Roosevelt was praised in newspaper editorials. Happy days, it seemed, were indeed returning.

★ ★ ★ ★ ★ ★ ★ ★ ★ ★ ★ ★ ★ ★ ★

Life in the Roosevelt White House was much like the New York Governor's Mansion. Louis Howe, and other advisors, moved in. The guest rooms were usually filled. The president and first lady occupied adjoining suites on the second floor. Missy's room was nearby. The Roosevelt children were grown now, but came for visits. There was a constant stream of visitors and general hubbub. Meals were chaotic affairs.

The president gave a press conference two days each week. He bantered with reporters, explaining new legislation and announcements so fluidly that one reporter quipped that

Roosevelt was "the best newspaperman who has ever been President of the United States."

Eleanor informed the nation that they should not expect their new first lady to be a symbol of elegance, but rather "plain, ordinary Mrs. Roosevelt." Despite this disclaimer, she immediately did things no first lady had ever done, including holding her own press conferences. Because of widespread discrimination facing female reporters, many of whom had been traditionally barred from presidential press conferences, Eleanor allowed only female reporters to attend her conferences.

She continued her role as a surrogate for her husband, traveling all over the United States, giving speeches for him and serving as his private investigative reporter. She also took on new writing projects, including two books, a collection of her father's letters and a tribute to him, and an assessment of the role of women in public life, entitled *It's Up to the Women*.

✳ ✳ ✳ ✳ ✳ ✳ ✳ ✳ ✳ ✳ ✳ ✳ ✳ ✳ ✳

On April 5, Roosevelt established the Civilian Conservation Corps, a government job creation program that put men to work planting trees and reclaiming land blighted by forest fires. This was a program dear to his heart because he believed it was the government's responsibility to preserve the environment. His years as assistant secretary of the navy had taught him to work a bureaucracy, and to get bills through Congress, so he had his program up and running in a surprisingly short time. By the end of June, the program had employed a quarter of a million men.

He gave his second Fireside Chat on May 7, and explained to the American people the need for the government to regulate things like minimum wages and hours in a workweek:

It's probably true that ninety percent of the cotton manufacturers would agree to eliminate starvation wages, would agree to stop long hours of employment . . . but what good is such an agreement if the other ten percent of cotton manufacturers pay starvation wages, require long hours, employ children in their mills and turn out burdensome surpluses? The unfair ten percent would produce goods so cheaply that the fair ninety percent would be compelled to meet the unfair conditions. Here is where the government comes in . . .

If the government required all employers to pay a fair minimum wage, he explained, then no company would be at a disadvantage for paying fair wages.

The debate over whether the United States should have a strong central government or a weak one dates back to the time of Alexander Hamilton and Thomas Jefferson. As Secretary of the Treasury, Hamilton looked for ways to create programs that would better the lives of the citizens. In the *Federalist Papers*, Hamilton commented that because people are creatures of habit, the more they become accustomed to having the government as part of their everyday lives, the more affection they will have for the government, in turn giving the government credibility and stabilizing the nation.

Later that month, he signed into law the Agricultural Adjustment Act, a farm bill regulating the agricultural industry, which, among other things, guaranteed farmers a fair price for the goods they produced. To enable people to stay in their homes even though they were unable to pay their mortgages, he urged Congress to pass the Homeowners Refinancing Act. He introduced the National Industrial Recovery Act of 1933, which, among other things, allowed workers to bargain collectively for better wages and working conditions. He used federal funds to build dams to

Jefferson, in contrast, believed that Hamilton's desire for a centralized government meant a loss of individual liberty. In his view, the entire reason the Revolutionary War had been fought was to free local governments from the tyranny of a distant, foreign, centralized government—and in Jefferson's view, anything outside of Virginia was foreign. Jefferson imagined the United States as a loose association of strong states. Hamilton, in contrast, believed a strong economy required the states working together in cohesion, which meant a strong central government.

provide water, which lowered the cost of water to Americans, and created jobs.

Initially, the Republicans were too shell-shocked by their land-slide loss in the presidential election to say or do much, but soon they were roused to anger. It became clear to them that Roosevelt was determined to dramatically increase the size of the federal government, and in doing so, he was also increasing the *power* of the central government. Conservatives denounced the New Deal as un-American and unconstitutional government control.

The National Recovery Act (NRA) adopted the emblem of the eagle. Roosevelt, in a Fireside Chat, asked all Americans to display the eagle as a badge of their support. He compared the badge to the bright patch soldiers wear on their backs so their comrades don't accidentally fire on them. Here a woman hangs an NRA poster in a restaurant window.

Roosevelt introduced so much legislation during his first three months in office that the period came to be known as the One Hundred Days. The legislation from the First One Hundred Days, and more that followed, came to be collectively called the New Deal.

During his first summer as president, Roosevelt asked Eleanor to investigate the situation in Appalachia, one of the poorest regions in the United States. When she returned, he listened to her reports of malnourished children and families unable to put

Roosevelt paid for his programs by increasing the national debt. One way governments raise money is by borrowing money, which a responsible government then spends in ways that create more jobs, goods, and services, thereby helping the nation's overall economy. If the money is well invested, the government sees a return on the investment, and is able to pay interest on the money it borrowed. Interest is the cost or fee of borrowing money, generally calculated as a percentage of the loan. Whoever lends money gets it back with interest. One way the government borrows money is to sell bonds, which offer a set interest rate over time. When the government pays the interest on the bonds, the investors earn money

The existence of a national debt has always been controversial. Alexander Hamilton said that "a national debt, if it is not excessive, will be to us a national blessing." Andrew Jackson, however, felt that debt was a great evil and made it one of his objectives as president to entirely eliminate the national debt. In 2018, America's national debt was approximately $21 trillion.

a real meal on the table. He immediately started looking for ways to send relief to Appalachia and other rural communities.

Roosevelt's critics derided his plan to offer assistance to needy people by arguing that government assistance encouraged laziness and forced those who were productive to support those who were not. In seeking to redistribute wealth (moving money from the upper classes to the lower classes), they called him a communist.

Roosevelt didn't think he was a communist. He believed he was saving the American economic system from itself by curbing its worst impulses and preventing it from becoming destructive. When the economy improved slightly, Roosevelt's critics insisted that it wasn't Roosevelt's legislation that had solved the problem. The only thing Roosevelt had done, they said, was restore confidence so that people would invest and trust banks again.

Many of Roosevelt's critics were the well-to-do who considered him a traitor to his class. After all, in the nineteenth century, low wages combined with the fact that nobody then paid income tax meant the affluent had been able to live like kings, while those at the bottom of the social ladder worked for starvation wages—a situation that many in the upper classes did not want to give up. J. P. Morgan, a successful financier and businessman, became so enraged by the very sight of Roosevelt's face that his family kept newspapers with pictures of Roosevelt away from him. A country club in Connecticut forbade mention of Roosevelt's name. One American who had been traveling extensively in the Caribbean confided, "During all the time I was gone, if anybody asked me if I wanted any news, my reply was always—'there is only one bit of news I want to hear and that is the death of Franklin D. Roosevelt. If he is not dead you don't need to tell me anything else.'" A former neighbor from the Hudson Valley so despised Roosevelt that he exiled himself to the Bahamas until Roosevelt was out of office.

Roosevelt responded to those who were hostile to his programs by laying out his philosophy of government:

> *In broad terms I assert that modern society, acting through its government, owes the definite obligation to prevent the starvation or dire want of any of its fellow men and women who try to maintain themselves but cannot . . . to those unfortunate citizens aid must be extended by government—not as a matter of charity but as a matter of social duty.*

He denounced the doubters as being divided into two groups: "those who seek special political privilege and second, those who seek special financial privilege."

By the end of 1933, the economy had stabilized enough so that it was no longer in a free fall. Recovery was still a long way off, but it was clear to most Americans that relief was at hand. Most Americans gave Roosevelt the credit for the recovery. He was enormously popular with laborers and farmers. In a Fireside Chat on June 28, 1934, he asked Americans to judge for themselves whether his programs were working when he asked, "Are you better off today than you were last year? Are your debts less burdensome? Is your bank account more secure?" The answer for most Americans was yes.

Roosevelt always insisted that in devising the New Deal, he was making things up as he went along. He said he was like the quarterback in a football game. After seeing how one play turned out, he called the next one. His guiding theory was: Do what works; abandon what does not. He denied that he was motivated by an ideology or a grand vision for America. While there was some truth in this—his program had a hit-or-miss and let's-experiment quality to it—one of his methods for dodging criticism was to refuse to be associated with particular ideology. One scholar argued that there was, in fact, an underlying principal guiding Roosevelt's New Deal: Roosevelt's core conviction that those in need are not free.

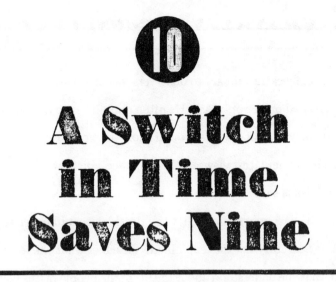

A Switch in Time Saves Nine

> *"Some people can never understand that you have to wait even for the best things, until the right time comes."*
>
> — *Franklin Delano Roosevelt*

t was an era in which most husbands expected their wives to be subservient. Eleanor, however, frequently took a public position contrary to her husband's. Once, for example, when she felt he was bowing to pressure from the business community to lower taxes and decrease spending, she wrote a column insisting that more public services were needed. The services would have to be paid for with taxes, she said, so people should just get used to that fact.

People understood she was admonishing her husband. What

was equally extraordinary to observers was how heavily the president relied on her opinions. He often quoted her to his cabinet. "You know my Missus gets around a lot," he would say, and then launch into her latest views. Or he'd preface a bit of wisdom with, "My Missus says . . . "

"She saw many things that the President could never see," Labor Secretary Perkins explained. "Much of what she learned and what she understood about the life of the people in this country rubbed off on [Roosevelt]. It could not have helped to do so because she had a poignant understanding." Perkins said people often gave the president credit for his intuitive understanding of laborers, but his intuition came from "his recollections of what she had told him."

One historian characterized Eleanor and Franklin's relationship as a "unique partnership that would help change the face of the country." Their youngest son said, "They were a team, and the Roosevelt years, I believe, were more fruitful and creative as a consequence of the partnership."

Not everyone approved of their unique partnership. Some despised Eleanor's political views. Others believed a wife belonged in the home. Among the critics was Sara Delano Roosevelt. Sara didn't think a wife should travel so much without her husband. She particularly disapproved of Missy fulfilling what Sara considered to be the central duties of a wife.

Missy was called a secretary, but in fact, she did the work that today we would call chief of staff, a high-ranking White House job. She was also a close personal friend of both the president and Eleanor. With Eleanor often traveling, it was Missy who catered to Franklin's moods, and arranged for evening social events. Missy sat with him when he needed company. When he wrote a letter in anger, Missy was the one who gently told him he should set it aside until his anger cooled. "Missy was the real wife," said one journalist. "She understood his nature perfectly, as they would say in a nineteenth-century novel." *Newsweek* praised Missy as the "President's Super-Secretary." Eleanor was grateful to Missy for taking care of all those matters so she was free to do her own work.

There was speculation at the time—and there has been speculation since—that Missy and Franklin had a romantic relationship. Eleanor didn't think so. Kathryn Smith, author of the only full-length biography about Missy LeHand, agreed. According to Smith, Roosevelt and Missy were extraordinarily close, worked well together, and had a high regard for each other—and that was it.

In addition to traveling widely and not minding her husband's friendship with Missy, Eleanor also shocked people by taking paying jobs as first lady. She wrote for publications and did commercial radio work. Her inheritance had shrunk considerably during the Depression, and the income from her paid work gave her the ability to do good for the public. She used all of her earnings for public works. Income from her radio work, for example,

Franklin, Eleanor, and Sara, 1931. In photographs, Franklin was careful to give the appearance that he had no physical disability.

allowed her to establish two places where unemployed girls who were searching for work could eat lunch and rest.

Eleanor had a dispute with the Secret Service when she told them that she didn't want to be accompanied by an agent everywhere she went. When the head of the Secret Service realized she wasn't going to budge, he insisted that she carry a gun with her. She asked one of Franklin's bodyguards to teach her to use it. "After considerable practice," she said, "I finally learned to hit a target. I would never have used it on a human being, but I thought I ought to know how to handle a revolver if I had to have one in my possession."

✶ ✶ ✶ ✶ ✶ ✶ ✶ ✶ ✶ ✶ ✶ ✶ ✶ ✶ ✶

Meanwhile, Roosevelt created the Securities and Exchange Commission (SEC), an independent agency of the federal government responsible for protecting investors by overseeing the money-lending industry and the sale of securities. (Securities are financial products that can be bought and sold, like loans, stocks, and bonds.)

The SEC issued regulations to stop the practice of investors manipulating the price of stocks for their own profit. The SEC also put an end to a similar practice known as insider trading, when people with access to private information about companies use that information to benefit from the market or manipulate the price of stock. To prevent a lending bubble, the SEC also passed laws to prevent banks from lending money to people who didn't have the ability to repay the loans. This was exactly the kind of regulation that proponents of laissez-faire economics despised.

To the chagrin of Roosevelt's critics, his popularity soared. The economy—while still a long way from complete recovery—ticked upward each year. The majority of Americans gave the credit to Roosevelt, and trusted him. In the midterm elections of 1934, the Republicans took another beating. As a result, the Democrats not only retained control of both houses of Congress, they picked up additional seats.

Roosevelt responded with even bolder measures: He enacted what has been called the Second New Deal, another flurry of legislation and programs that further strengthened the federal government while weakening the ability of business leaders and private organizations to control the government. He signed into law the Public Utility Holding Company Act of 1935, a law that allowed the government to regulate utilities like water and electricity to ensure low prices for consumers. He created the Social Security Administration, which functions like

Signing the
Social Security Act,
August 14, 1935

a government-sponsored pension and insurance: Workers and employers pay into Social Security with each paycheck, and when workers retire, they get a pension to help them live in their old age. He described Social Security as offering "to all a feeling of security as they look toward old age." Social Security also provided for a laborer's family if he was killed or injured and unable to work.

After the Social Security legislation was enacted, Eleanor visited West Virginia. Several men had recently been killed in a mining accident. One of the men who died received the Carnegie Medal posthumously because he'd gone into the mine to rescue others. Eleanor talked to his widow about how she and her children were going to manage. "I am going to get social security benefits of nearly sixty-five dollars," the widow explained. "I pay fifteen dollars a month on my house and land, and I shall raise vegetables and have chickens and with the money from the government I will get along very well." Eleanor reported back that Social Security was working.

In 1935, Roosevelt turned his attention to one of his pet projects, bringing electricity to poor rural areas. At the time, only 11 percent of American farms had electricity. In Mississippi, less than 1 percent of rural families had electricity.

Roosevelt's critics attacked his plan to bring electricity to Tennessee as a piece of communism on the grounds the federal government was taking over resources and redistributing wealth. Franklin used humor to avoid being pigeonholed into a political philosophy: "I tell them it is neither fish nor fowl, but whatever it is will taste awfully good to the People of the Tennessee Valley."

Critics of his New Deal legislation challenged his laws in court, arguing that the federal agencies he established were unconstitutional because, in issuing regulations and forming programs, the agencies (and president) were usurping states' rights and Congress's power to make laws.

The Supreme Court, consisting mostly of conservative justices, agreed. In May of 1935, the court struck down one of his programs, the National Industrial Recovery Act, as unconstitutional. The court ruled that in passing the law, Congress had delegated its law-making power to the president and executive branch. On January 6, 1936, the Supreme Court struck down Roosevelt's Agricultural Adjustment Act on the grounds that it was regulating matters that should be left to the states, and thus "invades the reserved power of the States."

In May, the Supreme Court struck down his Bituminous

There is nothing in the constitution specifically allowing for the kind of programs Roosevelt was creating. The Tenth Amendment to the Constitution defines the relationship of the states to the federal government:

> *The powers not delegated to the United States by the Constitution, nor prohibited by it to the States, are reserved to the States respectively, or to the people.*

The Constitution does, however, grant the federal government the authority to pass laws that "provide for the common defense and general welfare of the United States."

The question is how to interpret a vague phrase like "general welfare."

Alexander Hamilton—who was in favor of a strong central government—argued in his *Report on Manufactures* that the general welfare clause allowed for

Coal Conservation Act. Roosevelt knew if he didn't figure out a solution, the Supreme Court would undo every part of his New Deal.

any federal legislation that promoted the general welfare. James Madison and Thomas Jefferson—who were in favor of a weaker central government with more power residing in the states—said that such a broad reading of the clause would allow the federal government to do almost anything it wanted.

The first time the United States Supreme Court weighed in on this issue was in a challenge to Roosevelt's New Deal legislation. The Supreme Court agreed with Hamilton and said that Congress and the president could enact laws if they promoted the general welfare. The court said, though, that Roosevelt's legislation did not promote the general welfare, it only promoted the welfare in specific parts of the country.

The court thus struck down Roosevelt's legislation on the grounds that the legislation did not promote the general welfare, thus was unconstitutional under the Tenth Amendment.

★ ★ ★ ★ ★ ★ ★ ★ ★ ★ ★ ★ ★ ★ ★

leanor, meanwhile, had a new daily syndicated column entitled "My Day" in which she kept the public informed about her views and activities. She also took on the cause of civil rights for blacks. She made friends with Mary Jane McLeod Bethune, the daughter of former slaves in South Carolina. Bethune was working to make it possible for blacks to receive education. In an era when many people believed blacks and whites should be segregated, Eleanor made a point of sitting next to Bethune at a meeting of the National Council of Negro Women. Eleanor also befriended Walter Francis White, head of the NAACP, and lawyer Anna Pauline "Pauli" Murray, who would become one of the twentieth century's foremost advocates of women's rights and

Eleanor, Mary McLeod Bethune, and others at the opening of a Public Buildings Administration building, a dormitory for African American girls working for the government, 1943

black rights. When members of the NAACP wanted to get the attention of the president, they copied their letters to Eleanor.

Georgia Congressman Edward Cox issued a stern warning to the Democratic Party: If the Democratic Party took up the cause of black civil rights, white Southerners would abandon the party. Without white Southerners, quite simply, the Democrats would lose national elections.

Roosevelt heeded the warning. Eleanor, however, didn't have to worry about pleasing voters, so she was able to work on issues that would have been political suicide for an elected official. Roosevelt, however, quietly did what he could. He stayed away from the large, controversial issues, like segregation, but without fanfare, he undid some of the racist policies of his predecessors. He set aside Woodrow Wilson's segregation of government employees. He employed blacks in increasing numbers and at higher levels in federal service, including appointing a black judge in the Virgin Islands, the first African American to sit on a federal bench.

An aspect of the Eleanor-Franklin partnership, therefore, was while acting as the president's "eyes, ears, and legs," she was also able to embrace more radical positions. In the words of one historian, he was the politician; she was the agitator. As Eleanor become more vocal in support of black rights, people begged Roosevelt to silence his wife—but he never did. Once she asked him if he wanted her to stop. He told her to go right on ahead. "I can always say, 'well, that's my wife; I can't do anything about her.'"

By this time, President Roosevelt had won the support of most of America's African American population. One of the leading black newspapers, the *Baltimore Afro-American*, explained why blacks were abandoning the Party of Lincoln and declaring themselves Roosevelt Democrats:

> *Convinced by the fair play of President Roosevelt that*
> *the New Deal is for the colored man as well as the*
> *white, accepted in the Democratic Party and given more*
> *patronage in less than four years by Democrats than the*
> *Republicans gave them in fifty, colored citizens everywhere*
> *are now actively supporting and campaigning for*
> *America's truly liberal party, the Democrats.*

The NAACP strategy was to take what they could get from elected leaders like Roosevelt, and fight against segregation in federal courts, where judges were appointed for life and could thus do what they thought was right without having to worry about public opinion.

✱ ✱ ✱ ✱ ✱ ✱ ✱ ✱ ✱ ✱ ✱ ✱ ✱ ✱ ✱

Louis Howe's health had been gradually failing, and in August of 1935, he was moved from the White House to the U.S. Naval Hospital. Franklin and Eleanor visited him almost every day. He remained there for months. The night of April 18, 1936, he told a visitor, "Franklin is on his own now." Howe died later that night. Both Roosevelt and Eleanor were devastated by his death. "For one reason or another," Eleanor said later, "no one quite filled the void."

The election of 1936 would be Roosevelt's first campaign without Howe. He started campaigning early. He cast the election as a referendum on his programs. "There is one issue in this campaign," he said. "It is myself, and the people must be either for me or against me."

He felt confident. The economy was growing, slowly but surely. The national income had risen more than 50 percent since he'd taken office, and six million new jobs had been created. American banks were healthy and tightly regulated to prevent future problems. While only about half of Americans believed the Great Depression was over, he had the support of many more who admired and trusted him personally.

Having drawn African American support away from the

Republican Party for the first time since the Civil War, Roosevelt put together a new Democratic coalition that would make up the Democratic Party for the next fifty years: white Southerners, laborers, farmers, immigrants, and African Americans.

In June, the Republicans nominated Alfred Landon, governor of Kansas, as their presidential candidate. Landon had been a strong supporter of Theodore Roosevelt, but given the hostility among Republicans to Roosevelt and the New Deal, he was forced to campaign on an anti–New Deal platform, echoing the Supreme Court's criticism that Roosevelt was engaged in unconstitutionally enlarging the federal government.

Roosevelt campaigned vigorously, attacking those who wanted to return to the freewheeling, unregulated 1920s, calling them "economic royalists" and "the old enemies of peace . . . monopoly, speculation, reckless banking." He went on to say:

> *They are unanimous in their hate for me—and I welcome their hatred. I should like to have it said of my first administration that in it the forces of selfishness and lust for power met their match. I would like to have it said of my second administration that in it these forces met their master.*

He also mocked the way the Republicans had governed in the 1920s: "For twelve years this nation was afflicted with hear-nothing, see-nothing, do-nothing government" whose doctrine was "that government is best which is the most indifferent."

When the votes were counted on election night, Roosevelt was reelected with 61 percent of the vote—the largest since 1824, when popular votes were first tallied. He won every state except Maine and Vermont, giving him an electoral landslide.

✭ ✭ ✭ ✭ ✭ ✭ ✭ ✭ ✭ ✭ ✭ ✭ ✭ ✭ ✭

Roosevelt's victory gave him confidence—perhaps too much confidence. He was sworn in on January 20, 1937, becoming the first modern president inaugurated in January instead of March. He immediately turned his attention to his battle with the Supreme Court, which by then had ruled his New Deal legislation unconstitutional in seven of the nine challenges.

He asked Congress to give him authority to appoint additional justices to the Supreme Court—one for every justice then over the age of seventy, which would allow him to appoint six new justices, bringing the total of justices from nine to fifteen. His critics accused him of wanting to appoint justices who supported the New Deal. His proposal came to be called his court-packing scheme. He justified it by saying it would infuse the court system with "younger" justices who have "personal experience and contact with modern facts and circumstances . . . "

Criticism poured in from all sides. Republicans accused him of trying to usurp the judicial branch of government, after already usurping the legislative branch with his federal agencies. Even many Democrats accused him of overreaching. When the court-packing bill came up for a vote in Congress, the bill was defeated. The number of Supreme Court justices would remain at nine. The defeat was a deep embarrassment to the president who had just won an electoral landslide.

At about the same time, the Supreme Court began to shift, becoming less hostile to Roosevelt's legislation. Legal scholars still debate the reasons for the court's shift. Some believe that it was a result of Roosevelt's threats. Others argue that the court had been gradually shifting for some time, and the new attitude was just then becoming apparent. Others suggest that the president's landslide victory persuaded the justices to stop blocking his agenda. For whatever reason, in a move that came to be called "the switch in time that saved nine," the Supreme Court stopped overturning New Deal legislation.

In 1938—in what was to be the last of the far-reaching pieces of New Deal legislation—Roosevelt persuaded Congress to pass the Fair Labor Standards Act. The act established a national minimum wage, created a maximum forty-hour workweek, and abolished child labor. After the passing of the Fair Labor Standards Act, the Republicans regained enough strength to push back against Roosevelt's legislation. Labor strikes were leading to violence and again capturing headlines. The Republicans, who blamed the unrest on immigrants and those with radical communist ideas, were seen as tougher on immigration and tougher against the threat of communism. The result was that the Republican Party picked up more than seventy congressional seats and seven senate seats in the midterm elections.

Roosevelt no longer had any more time, anyway, to think about creating new federal programs. Alarming developments in Europe captured his full attention.

The Second World War

---

*"This generation of Americans
has a rendezvous with destiny."*

— Franklin Delano Roosevelt

n a stunning display of violence later called Kristallnacht—"Night of Broken Glass"—Nazi storm troopers
attacked the Jews of Germany. The riot was intended to
look like a spontaneous burst of fury, but, in fact, was
carefully planned. On the evening of November 9, 1938,
rioters went on a rampage of death and destruction. Jews were
attacked and killed in their homes. Jewish cemeteries were
desecrated. The windows of Jewish-owned shops were shattered. Almost three hundred synagogues throughout Germany

and Austria were burned while local firefighters stood by, watching.

For years, Hitler had been steadily passing laws against the Jews. He had revoked their German citizenship. They were forbidden to marry German citizens. They were deprived of the right to vote, and were required to carry special identification designating them as Jews. Hitler had already established concentration camps to imprison people he deemed to be enemies of Germany. The first two hundred concentration camp inmates were Communists. By late 1938, the Nazis were arresting Jews and other minorities and putting them into concentration camps.

Roosevelt issued the following statement in response to Kristallnacht: "The news of the past few days has deeply shocked public opinion in the United States." He added, "I myself could scarcely believe that such things could occur in a twentieth-century civilization." Not all Americans shared Roosevelt's loathing of the Nazis. Common in America in the 1930s—along with whites-only drinking fountains—were signs in hotels and restaurants restricting all ethnicities and minorities—blacks, Mexican Americans, Jews—with signs like: NO JEWS OR DOGS ALLOWED. There were Nazi-themed summer camps in America organized by the *Deutsche-Amerikanische Berufsgemeinschaft*

(German-American Alliance). In New York City on February 20, 1939, twenty thousand Americans rallied in support of Nazism in New York's Madison Square Garden. American Nazi sympathizers were a minority in America, but a vocal minority.

This Nazi march happened in New Jersey, July 18, 1937. Nearly one thousand uniformed men wearing swastika arm bands and carrying Nazi banners and the American flag paraded in New Jersey, sponsored by the New Jersey division of the German-American Bund.

On March 12, 1938, the Nazis marched into Austria, where they were greeted by many Austrians cheering and waving the Nazi flag. Hitler annexed Austria to his growing empire that he called the Third Reich. Next, the Nazis annexed a slice of the region then known as Czechoslovakia. Then they seized the remainder of Czechoslovakia. Hitler insisted that he needed to annex Czechoslovakia and Austria because of the large numbers of ethnic Germans living in those lands. He said the Germans— who he claimed were the most racially pure people in the world— didn't have the living space they deserved. Because Germany's neighbors would not willingly give up land, the Germans had to take it. After seizing Austria and Czechoslovakia, Hitler assured the rest of Europe and the world that he would stop there.

Hitler specifically promised Joseph Stalin, leader of the Soviet Union, that he would not attack Russia. Stalin believed Hitler's promise. Ignoring the advice of European leaders, he signed a nonaggression pact with Hitler, each promising not to attack the other.

Roosevelt was under no illusions about Hitler. He knew Hitler fully intended to continue expanding the Third Reich. Roosevelt also understood that Hitler's triumphs endangered democracy everywhere.

Italy—which had already invaded and taken over Ethiopia— now invaded and annexed Albania. Meanwhile, in Asia, Japan captured most of the major Chinese cities, including Shanghai. This attack allowed Japan to tighten its hold on Manchuria and Inner Mongolia, areas it had already conquered.

With extreme right-wing regimes growing more powerful and aggressive, Roosevelt invited King George VI of Great Britain and his wife to the United States as a symbolic gesture of American-British unity. The king accepted the invitation. The king and queen arrived in the United States on June 7, 1939. It was the first time a reigning British monarch ever set foot in America.

After a ceremonial reception in Washington, the Roosevelts and their royal guests retreated to Hyde Park. Prior to the visit, one of Sara's neighbors asked Sara if she intended to decorate

Roosevelt in conversation with the king, as Eleanor talks to the queen, June 8, 1939

in honor of the king and queen's visit. "Of course not," said Sara. "They're not coming to see a redecorated house. They're coming to see my house." The king and queen declared themselves charmed and impressed by their American hosts.

✴ ✴ ✴ ✴ ✴ ✴ ✴ ✴ ✴ ✴ ✴ ✴ ✴ ✴ ✴

On September 1, 1939, within a few months of the king and queen's visit, Hitler's armies invaded Poland, a country with very few ethnic Germans, so Hitler could have no justification for the invasion. Roosevelt learned of the attack when he was awakened at 2:50 a.m. and told the news. "It has come at last," he said. "God help us all."

Winston Churchill, future prime minister of England, had long been warning the British not to believe Hitler's promises, but the current prime minister, Neville Chamberlain, had insisted on a policy of appeasing Hitler. After Germany invaded Poland, Roosevelt wrote to Churchill, whom he had met long ago when he was serving as assistant secretary of the navy, saying, "I shall at all times welcome it if you will keep in touch with me personally with everything you want me to know about."

At 4:30 on the morning of September 3, 1939 Roosevelt was awakened and told that Britain and France had declared war on Germany. Later that day, he talked to Americans in a Fireside Chat. "Until four-thirty this morning," he said, "I had hoped against hope that some miracle would prevent a devastating war in Europe and bring to an end the invasion of Poland by Germany." He encouraged Americans to "maintain as a national policy the fundamental moralities, the teaching of religion and the continuation of effort to restore peace—for some day, though the time may be distant, we can be of even greater help to a crippled humanity."

The Nazis defeated the Polish army in just under a month, sparking a fierce debate in America between the isolationists— whose slogan was America First—and the interventionists. The isolationists believed America should mind its own business. The interventionists believed Hitler had to be stopped. Roosevelt was an interventionist, but the majority of American voters were isolationists. Roosevelt knew better than to move too far ahead of public opinion.

✦ ✦ ✦ ✦ ✦ ✦ ✦ ✦ ✦ ✦ ✦ ✦ ✦

The 1940 presidential election was approaching. The Constitution did not limit the number of terms a person could serve as president, but it had become an accepted norm for presidents to step aside after two terms. Roosevelt refused to say whether he would run for a third term. Even Eleanor had no idea what he planned to do. To a friend, he confided, "I do not want to run again unless between now and the convention things get very, very much worse in Europe." To put the matter simply, he didn't trust anyone else to fight the global rise of fascism.

On April 9, 1940, the war in Europe escalated when the Nazis invaded Denmark and Norway. Denmark was conquered in a matter of hours; Norway in June. Early morning on May 10, Germany attacked Belgium and the Netherlands. The Nazis began with a bombing blitz, followed by parachute drops and ground forces. The historic section of Rotterdam, a city in the Netherlands, was almost completely destroyed by German bombs. About nine hundred people were killed in the bombing of Rotterdam alone. Eighty-five thousand people were rendered homeless.

The night the Nazis attacked Belgium and the Netherlands, British Prime Minister Neville Chamberlain—whose strategy of appeasing Hitler was obviously failing—was forced to resign. King George asked Churchill to assume the duties of prime minister.

The Netherlands surrendered to Germany after five days of

fighting. The Nazis then advanced into France. Belgium fell to the Nazis on May 28. It wasn't long before the French army, believed to be the strongest in Europe, began crumbling. On June 10, when it was clear France would soon fall to the Nazis, Italy entered the war on Germany's side, primarily because Benito Mussolini, Italy's fascist ruler, wanted some of the spoils. Paris fell to the Nazis on June 14, and France surrendered on June 22.

★ ★ ★ ★ ★ ★ ★ ★ ★ ★ ★ ★ ★ ★

Roosevelt knew that the United States armed forces were no match for Nazi Germany. While the United States led the world in the manufacture of cars and household appliances, American armed forces was ranked sixteenth in the world, trailing Germany, Japan, France, England, Belgium, and Romania.

Roosevelt called on the United States to prepare to defend itself. He immediately met fierce resistance from the isolationists, the Nazi sympathizers, the anti-war pacifists, the mothers who lost sons in World War I, and others. The most influential of Roosevelt's critics was Charles Lindbergh, the famed aviator who, in 1927, had become the first solo pilot to fly nonstop across the Atlantic. Lindberg accused the British, the Jews, and Roosevelt of creating a "defense hysteria." He said the United States was in no danger unless Americans brought a Nazi invasion upon themselves by "meddling with affairs abroad." He also claimed that England was doomed, so it was in America's best interest to create an alliance with Hitler and the Nazis.

Lindbergh in the cockpit of an airplane, 1923

"If I should die tomorrow," Roosevelt privately told a friend, "I want you to know this. I am convinced Lindbergh is a Nazi." In public, Roosevelt warned against the perils of complacency. He assured the American people that he had no intention of sending American soldiers to die in European battlefields. At the same time, he pushed Congress to allow him to arm the nation. He got his way: Congress agreed to raise the debt ceiling so he could borrow money to mobilize for war. Money, though, wasn't enough. He needed factories to produce tanks, planes, and guns, and for that, he needed the cooperation of the nation's industrial leaders—the same people who had raged against him and his New Deal.

He assembled the National Defense Research Committee of business leaders to mastermind the mobilization effort. He lured industry leaders to cooperate with tax incentives. Some industrialists joined from patriotic duty. Some joined to make money. Others joined in the hopes that cooperation with Roosevelt would persuade him to overturn the parts of the New Deal they most hated.

The Chrysler and Ford auto plants were converted into airplane factories. Appliance factories were retooled to produce airplanes and military vehicles. With defense money flowing, government contracts were handed out, which created more jobs. It was the increased government spending in the effort to mobilize for war that finally lifted the United States entirely from the Great Depression.

✱ ✱ ✱ ✱ ✱ ✱ ✱ ✱ ✱ ✱ ✱ ✱ ✱ ✱ ✱

The date of the Democratic National Convention was approaching, but Roosevelt left the public in suspense about whether he planned to seek a third term. The convention opened on July 15, 1940. Roosevelt sent a message saying that he "had no wish to be a candidate again," and that "all the delegates to the convention are free to vote for any candidate."

When his message was read from the stage, the assembly was momentarily stunned. It slowly dawned on the delegates that Roosevelt hadn't said he would refuse the nomination. Just then, a loud voice boomed, "We want Roosevelt!" The crowd went wild.

"We want Roosevelt!"

"New York wants Roosevelt!"

"California wants Roosevelt!"

What followed was pure pandemonium. Roosevelt was thus nominated by acclamation. Unbeknownst to those gathered, the first shout of "We want Roosevelt!" had been planted by Edward Kelly, Chicago's mayor and one of Roosevelt's staunchest supporters. Kelly had been tipped off in advance about the contents of Roosevelt's message.

✱ ✱ ✱ ✱ ✱ ✱ ✱ ✱ ✱ ✱ ✱ ✱ ✱ ✱ ✱

One of the first things the Nazis did upon conquering a new nation was to begin rounding up Jews and other minorities, political enemies, homosexuals—anyone the Nazis believed were impure elements that should be removed from Europe. The captives were sent to concentration camps. Terrified refugees began arriving in the United States from Europe. Eleanor went to work behind the scenes, finding ways around the strict immigration quotas to allow more refugees into the country. Her work was frustrated when Roosevelt allowed immigration quotas to be tightened further after learning that members of the German military posing as tourists had infiltrated Western European countries prior to the Nazi invasion. The Germans posing as tourists then helped the Nazis during the invasion. These stories terrified lawmakers, who moved to prevent any immigrants—even refugees—from entering the nation.

Estimates vary as to how many European refugees were absorbed by America—but it's certain that large numbers were turned away. One boatful of Jewish refugees was denied admission to the United States, and was returned to Europe, where many met their deaths in Nazi concentration camps.

Meanwhile, Roosevelt did what he could to help Britain. He came up with a program called the lend-lease program whereby he sent military equipment to Britain. The idea was that Britain would pay America back later, when it could. He justified his program by drawing an analogy to a neighbor's house on fire. If your neighbor's house is on fire—he explained—you lend your neighbor a hose and worry about repayment later. Roosevelt's aim was to help the British beat the Nazis while keeping America from participating directly in the fighting. To get the supplies to Britain, American forces patrolled the Atlantic, a situation bound to escalate tensions between Germany and the United States.

On September 27, Japan, Italy, and Germany signed the Tripartite Pact, promising mutual assistance should any of the three be attacked. The purpose of the pact was to keep the United States out of the war.

* * * * * * * *

Roosevelt in his wheelchair on the porch of a Hyde Park estate cottage. In his lap is his dog, Fala, and Ruthie Bie, the granddaughter of a gardener who worked for the Roosevelt family.

The Republican nominee for president in 1940 was Wendell Willkie, a moderate Republican and industrialist, whose views were not far from

Roosevelt's. Both men supported a draft. Both men supported mobilizing for war, even though Roosevelt was seen as more likely to send soldiers to fight. The election was held on November 5, 1940. Roosevelt won with 55 percent of the popular vote—a decisive victory.

★ ★ ★ ★ ★ ★ ★ ★ ★ ★ ★ ★ ★ ★ ★

The nation's black leaders—including NAACP head Walter White and black labor union leader A. Philip Randolph—were enraged when black workers were unfairly passed over for defense jobs and were discriminated against in the armed forces. Roosevelt tried to duck the issue, but when the black leaders planned—and refused to call off—a march of tens of thousands in Washington, D.C., Roosevelt gave in. On June 25, 1941 he signed Executive Order 8802, banning discrimination in the defense industry and the federal government because of race, creed, color, or national origin.

When Roosevelt next tried to remove racial segregation in the armed forces, he ran into fierce opposition from his generals who warned him not to try such a thing during wartime. They insisted they could not prepare for war and integrate the armed forces at the same time. Roosevelt backed down. The civil rights leaders had to be content with Executive Order 8802, which they hailed as a victory. For the first time since the Reconstruction Era immediately after the Civil War, the federal government acted to guarantee equality for blacks.

✱　✱　✱　✱　✱　✱　✱　✱　✱　✱　✱　✱　✱　✱　✱

On June 22, 1941, the Nazi army, without warning, invaded the Soviet Union. Joseph Stalin, shocked, sprang into action. Initially, it looked like the Soviet army would quickly crumble under the Nazi invasion. But Stalin hurriedly prepared the nation for war, and the Soviet army regrouped. Stalin adopted a scorched-earth defense, destroying any supplies that might fall into German hands.

Stalin, the son of humble villagers, had joined the Communist Party as a young man. After the Russian Revolution, he was appointed to the office of general secretary of the Communist Party. He worked his way up through the party leadership. In the late 1920s, he seized control of the Soviet government. He immediately established a reign of terror, arresting his political rivals, conducting trials in which he declared his rivals "enemies of the people" and had them summarily executed. He succeeded in putting Russia on the road to industrialization, but his policies were brutal and resulted in millions of Russians forced into labor or starvation. As a result, numerous world leaders, including Churchill and Roosevelt, condemned Stalin's actions.

In August of 1941, during the height of the Nazi invasion of Russia, Churchill and Roosevelt met aboard the USS *Augusta* near Newfoundland.

"At last we have gotten together," Roosevelt said when they came face-to-face. He was standing up, holding his son Elliott's arm for support. Roosevelt and Churchill shook hands, and then had lunch. By the end of lunch, they were on a first-name basis. "I like him," Roosevelt wrote later, "and lunching alone broke the ice both ways . . . We talked of nothing but business, and reached a great measure of agreement on many points, both large and small."

They agreed to set aside longstanding American and British criticism of communism and Stalin, and ally themselves with Russia against the threat of fascism. They signed what later became known as the Atlantic Charter, a statement that included the right of all people to choose the form of government under which they will live. They also pledged to destroy Nazi tyranny.

✷ ✷ ✷ ✷ ✷ ✷ ✷ ✷ ✷ ✷ ✷ ✷ ✷ ✷ ✷

Sara Delano Roosevelt, eighty-six, was growing frail. She spent that summer at her Campobello summer house. In August, she returned to Hyde Park. She felt so weak that Eleanor went to Hyde Park to help her get settled. On Friday, September 5, Eleanor called Franklin at the White House and told him the end was near. He arrived at Hyde Park the following morning. He spent the day sitting with his mother. At 9:30 p.m., she lost consciousness. Franklin remained with her all night. The next day at about noon, when she drew her last breath, he was still by her side.

Several days later, Roosevelt, with help from his staff, was sorting through her possessions when one of his secretaries handed him a box he had never seen. Inside were several items carefully labeled in Sara's handwriting. Inside were Franklin's first pair of shoes, a lock of his baby hair, gifts he had made his mother when he was young, and his letters home from Groton and Harvard. Tears came to his eyes and he asked to be left alone. It was the only time his staff ever saw him cry.

✸ ✸ ✸ ✸ ✸ ✸ ✸ ✸ ✸ ✸ ✸ ✸ ✸ ✸ ✸

Six months after the Nazi invasion of Russia, the Soviet army launched a massive counterattack. The Germans had expected the Soviets to fall quickly and were not prepared for a winter campaign.

Meanwhile, Japan had occupied key airfields in Indochina. To punish Japanese aggression, the United States cut Japan off from oil and gas imports, which had a devastating effect on the Japanese. Many in Japan viewed the gas and oil embargo as an act of war, and felt further victimized by the West.

In November of 1941, Roosevelt received warnings that Japan was planning to attack the West. Hoping to prevent such an attack, Roosevelt sent the Emperor of Japan an appeal for peace and opened negotiations. The negotiations didn't go well. Many among the Japanese leadership believed that the Americans were not negotiating in good faith. One modern scholar argued that Roosevelt and his advisors didn't take the Japanese threat seriously enough. Many Americans indeed had inaccurate, stereotyped ideas of the Japanese. Certainly nobody expected the Japanese air fleet to attack America's strongest naval base located in Pearl Harbor on the Hawaiian island of Oahu.

Back to
the Hudson

*"The only limit to our realization
of tomorrow will be our doubts of today."*
— Franklin Delano Roosevelt

The day after Japan's devastating attack on Pearl Harbor, Roosevelt asked Congress for a declaration of war. Within hours, the House and Senate voted to declare war on Japan. Shocked by the attack, Americans rallied around the president. Even Charles Lindberg was in favor of war against Japan.

Three days later, Italy and Germany declared war on the United States.

In the bedlam and fury after war was declared, West Coast

military officials moved to intern the thousands of Japanese and Japanese Americans living on the West Coast. There was no evidence that any were disloyal. There was, however, evidence that for years, the Japanese on the West Coast had been unfairly discriminated against. "California was given by God to a white people," said the president of the Native Sons and Daughters of the Golden West, "and with God's strength we want to keep it as he gave it to us." Some of the racism was fueled by greed: Many Japanese were productive and successful. While Japanese farmed less than 1 percent of the cultivated land in California, they produced more than 40 percent of the state's crop. One vegetable shipper bluntly explained that the desire to get rid of the Japanese was "selfish." He added, "We might as well be honest."

False rumors that Japanese spies had given help with the attack on Pearl Harbor prompted a public outcry against people of Japanese heritage. Eleanor, Attorney General Francis Biddle, and others were strongly opposed to interning the Japanese. The president, however, deferred to the War Department. When the war department insisted, he signed the executive order for the internment. Eleanor, enraged by the decision, visited one of the camps to observe the conditions. She continued to voice her opposition to the internment all through the war.

Roosevelt, in a Fireside Chat, urged Americans out of their isolationism by walking them through a map and explaining that being surrounded by oceans didn't put them out of reach of enemies. "Those Americans who believed that we could live under the illusion of isolationism," he said, "wanted the American eagle to imitate the tactics of the ostrich." In other words, they had their heads buried in the sand—and Roosevelt wanted America to fly like an eagle.

* * * * * * * * * * * * * * *

By 1942 it was common knowledge that the Nazis were not merely rounding up the Jews and interning them in camp and treating them brutally: They were methodically and systematically killing them. The Nazis had tried to keep the genocide secret, but word leaked out. The mass killings were reported in American newspapers, but cautiously: During World War I, the newspapers had printed stories of atrocities, only to discover later that the stories had been incorrect.

When Roosevelt met with the heads of five major Jewish organizations, he confirmed that the information about the massacres was correct. The Jewish leaders then asked Roosevelt to "warn the Nazis that they will be held to strict accountability for their crimes." Roosevelt agreed to do so, while warning the Jewish leaders that "We are dealing with an insane man." He referred to Nazism as "a national psychopathic case," and said, "We cannot act toward them by normal means. That is why the problem is very difficult." He assured them that he'd do anything in his power to "be of service to your people in this tragic moment." Within days, at Roosevelt's request, Stalin and Churchill joined with him to issue a statement denouncing the massacre of the Jews.

The Nazi territories were impenetrable, making a major rescue operation impossible. On the theory that the way to save the Jews was to bring the war to a swift end, Roosevelt worked on stepping up production of tanks, planes, and weapons.

As early as 1939, America intelligence sources learned that the Germans were at work trying to create an atomic bomb. British scientists had also been trying to develop an atomic bomb, but had to stop research because of German air raids. Toward the end of 1942, Roosevelt authorized a group of scientists to set up research facilities to pick up the work where the British left off. The project to develop an atomic bomb was named the Manhattan Project, and was top secret.

★ ★ ★ ★ ★ ★ ★ ★ ★ ★ ★ ★ ★ ★ ★

R oosevelt, Stalin, and Churchill met in Tehran to discuss how to liberate Europe from the Nazis. They discussed the war—and celebrated Churchill's sixty-ninth birthday. "There were toasts and more toasts," one observer recalled. "One speech followed another." Stalin thanked Roosevelt for his lend-lease program that allowed the British to hold out against the Nazis. Without lend-lease, Stalin said, "we would lose the war." The three men talked late into the night. At 2:00 a.m., Roosevelt asked for the privilege of the last word.

"We have differing customs and philosophies and ways of life," he said. "But we have proved here at Tehran that the varying ideals of our nations can come together in a harmonious whole, moving unitedly for the common good of ourselves and the world."

The next day was given to detailed planning of the final stages of the war. When the three leaders left Tehran, Roosevelt and Churchill continued to Cairo, where they continued planning. They were ready now to invade Europe and liberate the Europeans from the Nazis. Churchill and Roosevelt agreed on the general who would lead the invasion: Dwight D. Eisenhower, a native of Texas who lived most of his life in Kansas, and would later serve as America's thirty-fourth president.

Bird's-eye view of the allied landing at Normandy

✦ ✦ ✦ ✦ ✦ ✦ ✦ ✦ ✦ ✦ ✦ ✦ ✦ ✦ ✦

O n June 6, 1944, later known as D-Day or the Normandy Invasion, about one hundred and sixty thousand Americans, British, and Canadian troops landed on a fifty-mile stretch of French beaches, on five separate beachheads. It was the largest amphibious military assault in history. The goal: To liberate Europe and put an end to Nazism.

About thirty-five hundred Americans were killed that day, and more than six thousand were wounded. German losses were much heavier. As the allies pushed into France, it was clear to everyone that the war had turned against the Germans.

By August, America and allied troops from Britain and Canada had liberated all of northern France. The British, Canadian, and American forces regrouped and prepared to march into the heart of Germany.

✦ ✦ ✦ ✦ ✦ ✦ ✦ ✦ ✦ ✦ ✦ ✦ ✦ ✦ ✦

N ot long after D-Day, Roosevelt signed the GI Bill offering financial assistance to returning veterans. Included in the benefits to returning soldiers was money to pay for a college education. Roosevelt explained the bill by saying, "I believe the nation is morally obligated to provide this training and education and the necessary financial assistance [to its veterans]." For the first time, returning soldiers would be provided government services.

1944 was the year of a presidential election. In July—during the height of the Battle of Normandy—Roosevelt announced that he would run for a fourth term. His health was failing, but with characteristic stubbornness and optimism, he refused to recognize that fact. He said he was reluctant to run. "All that is within me cries out to go back to my home on the Hudson River," he said, "but the future existence of the nation and the future existence of our chosen form of government are at stake."

Democratic Party leaders didn't quarrel with his choice to seek an unprecedented fourth term. The war was in the final stages. In the words of one Democrat, you don't change drivers while a car is speeding forward. But the Democratic Party leaders insisted that Roosevelt select Harry S. Truman, a senator from Missouri, as his vice presidential running mate. Because they knew Roosevelt's health was weakening, they understood that in selecting Roosevelt's vice president, they were selecting the next president of the United States.

Harry S. Truman started life as a farmer, and rose quickly in the Missouri Democratic Party. He was a strong supporter

Harry S. Truman, 1945

of Roosevelt's New Deal. When Roosevelt made bargains with the nation's industry to persuade factory owners to mobilize for war, Truman suspected that there was corruption in how defense contracts were handed out. He captured the hearts of his fellow Democrats when, as senator, he conducted an independent investigation into the handling of government defense contracts, uncovering and rooting out corruption among the industry's leaders.

Roosevelt's Republican challenger was Thomas Dewey, who had served three successive terms as New York's governor. Roosevelt wasn't planning to campaign, but when rumors were launched that he was too frail to serve as president, he went on a driving whistle-stop tour, giving speeches and posing for photographs.

When the votes were counted on election day, Roosevelt won with 25.6 million votes to Dewey's 22 million.

★ ★ ★ ★ ★ ★ ★ ★ ★ ★ ★ ★ ★ ★

he Roosevelts spent Christmas at Hyde Park. Anna and her husband, John, came with their three children; Franklin, Jr., and his wife arrived with their three children; Elliott was accompanied by his wife. James and John were on active duty. On Christmas Eve, Roosevelt read *A Christmas Carol* aloud to his grandchildren, who listened sprawled on the rug.

Eleanor and Franklin with their thirteen grandchildren, 1945

The next day, Roosevelt and Elliott drove around to inspect the estate. That evening, they had a long talk. Roosevelt revealed to his son that he felt lonely—Eleanor worked long hours and often traveled. He talked about how much he admired her strength of character and her value to him. "I only wish she wasn't so darned busy," he said. "I could have her with me much more if she didn't have so many other engagements."

Elliott took it upon himself to tell his mother that his father wished she could spend more time with him. "I hope this will come to pass," Eleanor replied.

✶ ✶ ✶ ✶ ✶ ✶ ✶ ✶ ✶ ✶ ✶ ✶ ✶ ✶ ✶

By the time of Roosevelt's fourth inauguration in January, it was clear the Germans wouldn't be able to fight much longer. In February, Roosevelt traveled to Yalta on the Crimean coast to meet again with Stalin and Churchill to discuss postwar Europe. The ideological split widened between Churchill and Roosevelt on one side, who wanted European nations to be free to choose democracy as their form of government, and Stalin on the other, who wanted as much of Europe as possible to embrace communism.

The three leaders agreed that Germany would be divided between West Germany, occupied by America and the Western allies, and East Germany, to be occupied by the Soviet Union. Stalin's armies had been pushing the Germans out of Poland and he'd been installing a pro-communist government in Poland, so

The "Big Three," Churchill, Roosevelt, and Stalin at the Yalta Conference. As Churchill pointed out, together these three men controlled three-quarters of all the air forces in the world, almost all of the world's navy, and directed combined armies of twenty million soldiers.

there was nothing Roosevelt or Churchill could do to stop him from occupying Poland. It was also clear that the United States would emerge from the war as a global economic and military superpower.

After Roosevelt returned to Washington, he felt tired all the time, even in the morning after a full night of sleep. Sometimes he nodded off while reading his mail. His skin grew pallid with a bluish tint. At the end of the month, he went with several companions to Warm Springs, hoping to recoup his strength. Among his guests was Lucy Mercer, the secretary he'd been in love with years earlier. Lucy now went by her married name, Lucy Rutherfurd. Also with them were a few of Roosevelt's cousins, some of his aides, and a portrait painter who was a friend of Lucy's.

Just before lunch on April 12, Roosevelt was having his portrait painted when he complained of a headache. Moments later he collapsed from a massive stroke. He never regained consciousness, and died several hours later.

Eleanor received word that she must come to Warm Springs immediately. She flew to Georgia, arriving in Warm Springs just after midnight. Shortly after she arrived, one of Franklin's cousins told her that Lucy Mercer had been in the room with Franklin when he died. Eleanor responded by asking to be alone for a few minutes. Later the cousin justified telling Eleanor such a thing at such a moment by saying Eleanor would have found out eventually. When Eleanor rejoined the others, her expression was resolute. She intended to keep her pain and humiliation to herself.

The next morning, Eleanor rode the funeral train with

Roosevelt's funeral procession was viewed by over five hundred thousand mourners.

Franklin's body. The coffin bearing his body was propped up by

a window. As the train moved slowly toward Washington, D.C.,

hundreds of thousands of people lined the tracks, many dressed

in black. Eleanor's five children—and large crowds—were waiting

in Washington. A memorial service was held in the East Room of

the White House. After that, Roosevelt's coffin—with his family

in attendance—was put back on the train. The train carried his

body northward, back to the Hudson, for burial on the grounds

of his boyhood home in Hyde Park.

Afterward

n April 25, 1945, Benito Mussolini, head of the Italian Fascist Party, knew the Italians were about to lose the war, so he tried to flee to Switzerland. He was assassinated by domestic enemies before he could make it to the border, putting an end to his fascist regime. Hitler received news of Mussolini's death as the Soviets were advancing toward Berlin. Not wanting to give his enemies the satisfaction of killing him, Hitler committed suicide in his underground bunker on April

30 by swallowing a capsule of cyanide and shooting himself in the head.

On May 7, 1945, Germany surrendered to the allies, bringing the war in Europe to an end. When allied soldiers liberated the Nazi concentration camps, they uncovered the unspeakable horrors of genocide. By some estimations, the Nazis systematically murdered as many as eleven million men, women, and children. Six million of the slain were Jews, wiping out almost the entire European Jewish population.

The horrors of the Nazi genocide persuaded many that Roosevelt had been right in recognizing the dangers of fascism. The genocide caused public opinion to turn sharply against groups such as the Ku Klux Klan, white nationalists, and proponents of America First. White supremacists in the United States, though, did not give up their belief in the superiority of the white race. Their movement was discredited—but they didn't go away. They went underground, and remained a powerful force on the fringes of American politics.

By the end of the summer, Japan's defeat, too, was imminent— but the Japanese wouldn't surrender. When the new president, Harry S. Truman, was advised that a land invasion of Japan would cost ten times the number of American lives as the Normandy invasion, he decided against a Japanese D-Day. Instead, he forced Japan to surrender by dropping the world's first atomic bomb on Hiroshima, killing an estimated eighty thousand civilians. When the Japanese still did not surrender, he ordered a second atomic bombing of Nagasaki. The next day, Japan surrendered, bringing World War II to a devastating end.

★　★　★　★　★　★　★　★　★　★　★　★　★　★

When the Republicans gained a majority in Congress after the 1946 elections, they introduced a constitutional amendment to limit a president to two elected terms, or a maximum of ten years in office. The amendment, which became part of the Constitution in 1951, was partly intended as a posthumous rebuke of Roosevelt. The amendment, though, ensures that Roosevelt will remain the only president to serve longer than ten years, and guarantees him a place in history as America's longest-serving president.

Legacy

hen Roosevelt took office, America was a minor military power in the grip of its most devastating economic depression. By the end of Roosevelt's years in office, America was greater "than any power since the Roman Empire. And it had a central government commensurate with that role." It was Franklin Delano Roosevelt who enlarged the power of the federal government and lifted the nation from near ruin to global leadership.

The New Deal changed the relationship of ordinary

Americans to the federal government. After Roosevelt, people grew accustomed to looking to the government for basic protections and guarantees, including the right to a living wage and security in old age. Social Security changed the lives of working Americans by guaranteeing that they would not starve or find themselves homeless when they were no longer able to work.

The GI Bill was among the most far-reaching of Roosevelt's programs. The bill helped millions of veterans obtain a college education, lifting a segment of the population by offering them a higher education, which in turn opened up the opportunity for better jobs. Essentially, the GI Bill educated a generation and moved a large segment of Americans out of poverty and into the middle class.

The New Deal, however, caused an ideological crisis for the many Americans opposed to a powerful central government. Republicans, in particular, have struggled ever since to come to terms with the America created by Roosevelt's New Deal legislation. Numerous conservative candidates since Roosevelt's time have run for office on a promise to repeal Social Security. They discovered that overturning such programs isn't easy. People may dislike the idea of a welfare state, but once they have benefits like

Social Security, minimum wage, and unemployment insurance, they don't want to give them up.

✶ ✶ ✶ ✶ ✶ ✶ ✶ ✶ ✶ ✶ ✶ ✶ ✶ ✶ ✶

Eleanor spent the remainder of her life fighting for the causes she believed in. President Truman called her the First Lady of the World, and appointed her to the United Nations General Assembly, where she served as chair of the Human Rights Commission. Shortly after she left her position in the United Nations, the Supreme Court overturned *Plessy v. Ferguson*, making racial segregation illegal in the United States, and igniting the modern civil rights movement. Eleanor joined the NAACP Board of Directors, and used her influence to advance the cause of racial equality. When Democrat John F. Kennedy was elected president in 1960, he reappointed her to the United Nations.

The First Lady of the World died on November 7, 1962. She is buried alongside her husband, Franklin Delano Roosevelt, in the Rose Garden at Hyde Park.

Selected Writings of Franklin D. Roosevelt

*Excerpts from Roosevelt's
First Inaugural Speech,
March 4, 1933, delivered
when America was in the throes
of the Great Depression.*

. . . This great nation will endure, as it has endured, will revive and will prosper. So, first of all, let me assert my firm belief that the only thing we have to fear is fear itself—nameless, unreasoning, unjustified terror which paralyzes needed efforts to convert retreat into advance. In every dark hour of our national life, a leadership of frankness and of vigor has met with that understanding and support of the people themselves which is essential to victory. And I am convinced that you will again give that support to leadership in these critical days.

In such a spirit on my part and on yours we face our common difficulties. They concern, thank God, only material things. Values have shrunken to fantastic levels: taxes have risen; our ability to pay has fallen; government of all kinds is faced by serious curtailment of income; the means of exchange are frozen in the currents of trade; the withered leaves of industrial enterprise lie on every side; farmers find no markets for their produce; and the savings of many years in thousands of families are gone. More important, a host of unemployed citizens face the grim problem of existence, and an equally great number toil with little return. Only a foolish optimist can deny the dark realities of the moment.

And yet our distress comes from no failure of substance. We are stricken by no plague of locusts. Compared with the perils which our forefathers conquered, because they believed and were not afraid, we have still much to be thankful for. Nature still offers her bounty and human efforts have multiplied it. Plenty is at our doorstep, but a generous use of it languishes in the very sight of the supply.

Primarily, this is because rulers of the exchange of mankind's goods have failed, through their own stubbornness and their own incompetence, have admitted their failure, and abdicated. Practices of the unscrupulous money changers stand indicted in the court of public opinion, rejected by the hearts and minds of men.

True, they have tried. But their efforts have been cast in the pattern of an outworn tradition. Faced by failure of credit, they have proposed only the lending of more money. Stripped of the lure of profit by which to induce our people to follow their false leadership, they have resorted to exhortations, pleading tearfully for restored confidence. They only know the rules of a generation of self-seekers. They have no vision, and when there is no vision the people perish . . .

Happiness lies not in the mere possession of money; it lies in the joy of achievement, in the thrill of creative effort. The joy, the moral stimulation of work no longer must be forgotten in the mad chase of evanescent profits. These dark days, my friends, will be worth all they cost us if they teach us that our true destiny is not to be ministered unto but to minister to ourselves, and to our fellow men . . .

Letter written from Roosevelt to Albert Einstein, after receiving a letter explaining that Professor Einstein felt he understood how to build an atomic bomb

October 19, 1939

My dear Professor:

I want to thank you for your recent letter and the most interesting and important enclosure.

I found this data of such import that I have convened a Board consisting of the head of the Bureau of Standards and a chosen representative of the Army and Navy to thoroughly investigate the possibilities of your suggestion regarding the element of uranium.

I am glad to say that Dr. Sachs will cooperate and work with this Committee and I feel this is the most practical and effective method of dealing with the subject.

Please accept my sincere thanks.

An Excerpt from Roosevelt's Campaign Address at Cleveland, Ohio on November 2, 1940; World War II had begun in Europe

It is the destiny of this American generation to point the road to the future for all the world to see. It is our prayer that all lovers of freedom may join us–the anguished common people of this earth for whom we seek to light the path.

I see an America where factory workers are not discarded after they reach their prime, where there is no endless chain of poverty from generation to generation, where impoverished farmers and farm hands do not become homeless wanderers, where monopoly does not make youth a beggar for a job.

I see an America whose rivers and valleys and lakes–hills and streams and plains–the mountains over our land and nature's wealth deep under the earth–are protected as the rightful heritage of all the people.

I see an America where small business really has a chance to flourish and grow.

I see an America of great cultural and educational opportunity for all its people.

I see an America where the income from the land shall be implemented and protected by a government determined to guarantee to those who hoe it a fair share in the national income.

An America where the wheels of trade and private industry continue to turn to make the goods for America. Where no businessman can be stifled by the harsh hand of monopoly, and where the legitimate profits of legitimate business are the fair reward of every businessman–big and little–in all the Nation.

I see an America with peace in the ranks of labor.

An America where the workers are really free and–through their great unions undominated by any outside force, or by any dictator within–can take their proper place at the council table with the owners and managers of business. Where the dignity and security of the working man and woman are guaranteed by their own strength and fortified by the safeguards of law.

An America where those who have reached the evening of life shall live out their years in peace and security. Where pensions and insurance for these aged shall be given as a matter of right to those who through a long life of labor have served their families and their nation as well.

I see an America devoted to our freedom–unified by tolerance and by religious faith–a people consecrated to peace, a people confident in strength because their body and their spirit are secure and unafraid . . .

Timeline

1882   ✶ JANUARY 30: Franklin Delano Roosevelt (FDR) is born in Hyde Park.

1896   ✶ FDR enters Groton.

1900   ✶ FALL SEMESTER: FDR begins his studies at Harvard.

       ✶ DECEMBER 8: FDR's father dies.

1905   ✶ MARCH 17: FDR marries Eleanor Roosevelt.

1906   ✶ MAY 3: Anna Roosevelt is born.

1907   ✶ DECEMBER 23: James Roosevelt is born.

1909   ✶ MARCH 18: Franklin Delano Roosevelt Junior (the first) is born.

       ✶ NOVEMBER 5: He dies just short of eight months old.

1910   ✶ 5 SEPTEMBER 23: Elliott Roosevelt is born.

       ✶ NOVEMBER 8: FDR is elected to the New York Senate.

1912   ✶ FDR is reelected to the New York Senate.

1913   ✶ MARCH 17: FDR is sworn in as assistant secretary of the navy.

1914   ✶ JUNE 28: Archduke Ferdinand and Archduchess Sophie are assassinated, sparking the outbreak of World War I.

       ✶ AUGUST 17: Franklin Delano Roosevelt Junior (the second) is born.

1916   ✶ MARCH 13: John Roosevelt is born.

       ✶ NOVEMBER 7: President Woodrow Wilson is reelected.

1917 ✶ FEBRUARY 3: Germany sinks the SS *Housatonic*.

✶ APRIL 2: The United States enters World War I

1918 ✶ NOVEMBER 11: World War I ends.

1920 ✶ JULY 6: FDR becomes James Cox's vice presidential running mate in the 1920 election.

✶ NOVEMBER 2: Cox and Franklin are defeated by Warren G. Harding and Calvin Coolidge.

1921 ✶ FDR contracts Polio while vacationing at Campobello, New Brunswick, Canada.

1924 ✶ JULY: FDR nominates Governor Al Smith for president at the Democratic National Convention in New York.

✶ OCTOBER: Visits Warm Springs, Georgia, for the first time.

1928 ✶ OCTOBER 2: New York State Democratic Party nominates FDR for governor.

✶ NOVEMBER 6: FDR is elected governor of New York.

1929 ✶ OCTOBER 29: Black Tuesday, the stock market crash ushers in the Great Depression.

1930 ✶ NOVEMBER 4: FDR is reelected governor of New York.

1932 ✶ JUNE: FDR is nominated for president of the United States at the Democratic Convention in Chicago.

✶ NOVEMBER 8: FDR defeats Herbert Hoover and is elected the thirty-second President of the United States.

1933 ✶ JANUARY 30: Hitler becomes chancellor of Germany.

✶ MARCH 4: FDR is inaugurated president of the United States.

✶ MARCH: FDR begins enacting his New Deal legislation.

1934 ✶ In the midterm elections, Democrats strengthened their majorities in both the House and Senate.

1936 ✶ APRIL 18: Louis Howe dies.

✶ NOVEMBER 3: FDR is reelected for a second term.

1937 ✶ JANUARY 20: FDR is inaugurated to his second term.

✶ FEBRUARY 5: FDR asks for legislation allowing him to appoint six more Supreme Court justices.

✶ JULY 20: Congressional leaders reject FDR's "court-packing" scheme.

1938 ✶ NOVEMBER 9–10: Nazis terrorize German Jews in Kristallnacht, the Night of Broken Glass.

1939 ✶ JUNE: FDR and Eleanor entertain the King and Queen of Great Britain.

✶ SEPTEMBER 1: Nazi Germany attacks and occupies Poland.

1940 ✶ APRIL–MAY: Germany invades Belgium, the Netherlands, Luxembourg, and France.

✶ JULY 17: FDR accepts the Democratic Party's nomination for an unprecedented third term.

✶ SEPTEMBER 27: Japan, Germany, and Italy sign a pact pledging mutual assistance in war.

✶ NOVEMBER 5: FDR is reelected to a third term.

1941 ✶ JANUARY 20: FDR is inaugurated to his third term.

✶ JUNE 22: Germany invades Russia.

✶ AUGUST 9–12: Churchill and Roosevelt meet at Argentia Bay in Newfoundland.

Timeline

* **SEPTEMBER 7**: Sara Delano Roosevelt dies at the age of 86.

* **DECEMBER 7**: Japan attacks Pearl Harbor, America enters World War II.

1943
* **NOVEMBER 28–DECEMBER 2**: FDR, Churchill, and Stalin meet in Tehran to discuss the invasion of Europe.

1944
* **JUNE 6**: The Normandy Invasion begins.

* **JULY 21**: FDR is nominated for a fourth term as president.

* **SEPTEMBER 12**: Allied forces enter Germany.

* **NOVEMBER 7**: FDR is elected to a fourth term.

1945
* **APRIL 12**: FDR dies in Warm Springs, Georgia.

Notes

Prologue:
America Under Attack

4 "I was . . . in itself was exhausting": Eleanor Roosevelt, *Autobiography*, 226.

4 "Put him on . . . No!": Persico, xxiv.

4–5 "Deadly calm": Goodwin, 289.

6 "His reaction to any great . . . never the slightest emotion that was allowed to show": Ward, *Before the Trumpet*, location 12785.

6 "We haven't got the navy . . . before we can have a victory": Goodwin, 289.

7 sledding on the banks of the Hudson River: Goodwin, 13. This incident comes from an interview the author had with Betsey Cushing Whitney, FDR's daughter-in-law (she was the first wife of his son James).

1. Always Bright and Happy

8 "All that is in me goes back to the Hudson": Lash, 116.

9 "Even as a little mite . . . sea-faring man": Sara Delano Roosevelt, *My Boy Franklin*, 31.

10 "In thinking back to my earliest days . . . places and people": Ward, *Before the Trumpet*, location 2187.

10–11 "Then with a curious little gesture . . . Oh, for freedom": Sara Delano Roosevelt, *My Boy Franklin*, 5.

11 "We could only deduce . . . back to his routine": Sara Delano Roosevelt, *My Boy Franklin*, 5–6.

12 "had a gift for saying the right thing . . . several languages": Smith, location 181.

13   "I will not say that all Democrats are horse thieves, but it would seem that all horse thieves are Democrats": Burns, location 236–247.

14   "a very nice child . . . always bright and happy": Ward, *Before the Trumpet*, location 2253–2254.

16   "I'm not sure I like boys who think too much . . . we could do without": Ward, *Before the Trumpet*, location 7888.

16   "The best thing for a boy . . . bed and to sleep": Ward, *Before the Trumpet*, location 3562.

16   "man to man": Ward, *Before the Trumpet*, location 3356.

17   "entirely out of things": Ward, *Before the Trumpet*, location 3598.

18   "dry-eyed" and "resolute": Ward, *Before the Trumpet*, location 3435.

18   "I am getting on very well with the fellows although I do not know them all yet": *F.D.R. Letters,* Early Years, 42.

18   "I am very well": *F.D.R. Letters,* Early Years, 44.

20   "desperately lonely and wildly furious": Cook, 71.

20   "shy and solemn child . . . lacking the spontaneous joy of youth": Goodwin, 92.

21   "Cousin Eleanor has a very good mind": Ward, *Before the Trumpet*, location 6140.

22   "very delicate and tired-looking . . . sweet to be together": Ward, *Before the Trumpet*, location 4463.

2. Anna Eleanor Roosevelt

24   "To reach a port, we must . . . not drift": Roosevelt, *Fireside Chats,* April 14, 1938.

27   "I can be President . . . I cannot possibly do both": Gould, *Bull Moose*, 139–140.

27   King, "History of the Teddy Bear": Smithsonian.com.

28–29 "The effort to become his own man . . . maneuver he brought to the White House": Ward, *First-Class Temperament*, hardcover flap copy.

30   "influenced others . . . comes in contact with": Lash, 91.

30   "E is an Angel" . . . "Lunch with Aunt K's party" . . . "After
     lunch . . . with my darling": Cook, 132.

32   "When he told me he loved me . . . I loved him too": Goodwin, 97.

32   "Franklin gave me quite a startling announcement": Lash, 109.

33   "Dearest Mama . . . who love you": Ward, *Before the Trumpet*,
     location 5295.

33   "I know just how you feel . . . love me a little": Ward, *Before the
     Trumpet*, location 5302.

34   "Franklin's feelings did not change": Eleanor Roosevelt,
     Autobiography, 41.

37   "a wonderful playmate . . . a lot of things": Ward, *First-Class
     Temperament*, location 13,927.

38   "I had never been in a county clerk's office . . . full-fledged lawyer":
     Ward, *First-Class Temperament*, location 1544.

38   "Everyone . . . adolescent in its buoyancy": Ward, *First-Class
     Temperament*, location 1627.

39   "Anyone who is governor . . . with any luck": Ward, *First-Class
     Temperament*, location 1958.

39   "engaging frankness" and "sincerity": Ward, *First-Class
     Temperament*, location 1957.

39   "in any way mine . . . represent the way I wanted to live": Eleanor
     Roosevelt, *Autobiography*, 61.

40   "absorbing the personalities . . . dominate me": Eleanor Roosevelt,
     Autobiography, 61.

3. Entering Politics

42   "There are many ways of going forward, but only one way of
     standing still": As quoted in the *Congressional Record*, Vol. 154,
     Part 16, 2915, 9-29-2008. Widely attributed to Franklin D.
     Roosevelt.

Notes

42 "I listened to . . . my only mission in life": Eleanor Roosevelt, *Autobiography*, 63.

43 "for so fine a young man to associate with 'dirty' politicians": Ward, *First-Class Temperament*, location 2298–2309.

43 "My father and grandfather . . . the Democratic candidates": Lash, 170.

48 "I am pledged to no man . . . so I shall remain": Burns, location 775.

48–49 "that little ring of Republican . . . good government": Burns, location 774.

50 "my friends": Ward, *First-Class Temperament*, location 2246.

50 "When I see you again . . . you will": Ward, *First-Class Temperament*, location 2502.

50 "I had a particularly . . . we had a joyous campaign": Smith, location 1541.

52 "You know . . . awfully mean cuss when I first went into politics": Ward, *First-Class Temperament*, location 3420.

54 "That dirty little man": Jenkins, 550.

54 "political sagacity": Lash, 212.

55 "He had a youthful lack of humility . . . the common lot": Smith, location 1825–1833.

55 "government regulation . . . old fogeys will cry out 'well done'": Smith, location 1925.

56 "We are for liberty, but we are for the liberty of the oppressed": Burns, location 1052.

57 "I am fighting . . . closed doors of opportunity": Burns, location 1052.

59 "How would you like . . . anything in the world": Burns, location 1063.

59 "our kind of liberal": Lash, 224.

60 "You know the Roosevelts, don't you . . . he wishes to ride in front": Persico, 6.

4. Assistant Secretary of the Navy

61 "Happiness lies in the joy of achievement, in the thrill of creative effort": Roosevelt's first Inaugural Address, delivered March 4, 1933.

61 "My only regret is that you couldn't have been here with me": *Eleanor Roosevelt*, 201.

63 "I get my fingers into everything, and there's no law against it": Ward, *First-Class Temperament*, location 4469.

63 "I want you all to feel . . . we can talk matters over": Ward, *First-Class Temperament*, location 5029.

64 "brilliant, lovable . . . the life of the party": Ward, *First-Class Temperament*, location 4686.

64 "*very* big job . . . so unreadable": Lash, 225.

65 "personal insult and humiliation": Smith, location 2268.

68 "A complete smashup is inevitable": Smith, location 2722.

68–69 "The best that can be expected . . . I think unlikely": Smith, location 2741

69 "As I expected . . . to be enacted": Burns, location 61.

69 "bewildered by it all, very sweet but very sad": Burns, location 60.

72 "good fight": Smith, location 2796.

73 "wanton murder": Smith, location 2889.

73 "The President does not want to rattle the sword": Ward, *First-Class Temperament*, location 6720.

74 "For ten years . . . restricted during this period": Eleanor Roosevelt, *Autobiography*, 61.

5. The Great War

76 "Courage is not the absence of fear, but rather the assessment that something else is more important than fear": From a speech FDR wrote before he died, but never delivered. On display at the FDR Library in Hyde Park.

77 Do *please* get through two vital things *today* . . . if we are to go ahead. Roosevelt": Ward, *First-Class Temperament*, location 7668.

77 "women in Washington paid no more . . . meet the unusual demand of wartime": Eleanor Roosevelt, *Autobiography*, 87.

79 "debonair": Ward, *First-Class Temperament*, location 6789.

86 "I have seen . . . agony of mothers and wives. I hate war": Ward, *First-Class Temperament*, location 8410–8420.

87 "The bottom dropped . . . I really grew up that year": Lash, 270.

88 "I can forgive . . . but I cannot forget": Smith, location 3574.

88 "We have made partners . . . privilege and right?": Quotation available here: www.senate.gov/artandhistory/history/minute /A_Vote_For_Women.htm.

89 "The right of citizens of the United States to vote . . . enforce this article by appropriate legislation": United States Constitution, full text available here: www.law.cornell.edu/constitution/overview.

90 "My cousin's death . . . leaving that he was better": Ward, *First-Class Temperament*, location 9038.

6. Trial by Fire

94 "The test of our progress . . . for those who have too little": Roosevelt's second Inaugural Address, delivered January 20, 1937.

96 "The progressive movement . . . Yesterday it died": Burns, location 1477.

96–97 "The young man whose name . . . conjure with American politics: Franklin D. *Roosevelt*": Ward, *First-Class Temperament*, location 10850.

98 "I miss . . . with me in all these doings": Ward, *First-Class Temperament*, location 11690. Ward suggested that Franklin wanted her at his side because it was the first year that women were allowed to vote in presidential elections, and he thought her presence would help appeal to women voters.

Notes

98 "I was flattered . . . a range of topics": Eleanor Roosevelt, *Autobiography*, 110.

100 "I never quite felt that way before": Smith, location 4205.

100 "I tried to persuade myself . . . collapsed as well": Smith, location 4205.

101 "He looked very strained . . . completely calm": Ward, *First-Class Temperament*, location 12793.

102 "very slow recovery . . . slight power to twitch the muscles": Ward, *First-Class Temperament*, location 13170.

102 "He has such courage . . . without crushing him": Ward, *First-Class Temperament*, location 13194.

103 "perfect naturalness with which the children accepted his limitations": Eleanor Roosevelt, *Autobiography*, 141–142.

109 "He has a personality . . . Alfred E. Smith": Ward, *First-Class Temperament*, location 14993.

109 "The crowd just went crazy . . . stupendous": Ward, *First-Class Temperament*, location 15006.

111 "not much beyond . . . pretty run-down": Goodwin, 116.

112 "We didn't like her one bit. She ruined every maid we ever had": Ward, *First-Class Temperament*, location 16651.

112 "I can still remember the day . . . collapse from exhaustion": Goodwin, 116.

113 "My own legs continue to improve . . . It is still a mystery to me as to why that left knee declines to lock": Burns, location 1779.

7. The Great Depression

115 "Take a method . . . try something": Smith, location, 5797.

116 "When you're in politics, you have to play the game": Ward, *First-Class Temperament*, location 17119.

117 "something pathetic . . . Franklin D. Roosevelt": Smith, location 4967.

118 "A governor doesn't have to be an acrobat . . . brainwork": Smith, location 4967.

118 "I am counting on my friends from all over the state to help me walk in": Smith, location 4957–4972.

119 "It's not over by a long shot": Smith, location 4999.

121 "The polio was very instrumental in bringing them much closer in a very real partnership": Goodwin, 98.

121 "It is my firm . . . would never have come about": Smith, location 5147.

122 "You felt he was talking to you, not 50 million others but to you personally": Goodwin, 58.

127 "people felt that the ground under their feet was giving way": Rauchway, 19.

8. A New Deal

129 "We have always known that heedless . . . bad economics": Widely attributed to Franklin Delano Roosevelt. Quoted here from the *Congressional Record,* vol. 154, Part 16, page 22915, September 28, 2008.

130 "If the farmer starves today . . . tomorrow": Smith, location 5328.

130 "If Thomas Jefferson were alive he would be the first to question this concentration of economic power": Smith, location 5339.

130 "Never let your opponent . . . fight all by himself": Smith, location 5357.

131 "I do not see how Mr. Roosevelt . . . raise a finger to bring it about": Smith, location, 5511.

133 "health and powers of endurance are such as to allow him to meet any demand of private and public life": Smith, location 5668.

136 "Liberal thought . . . a new deal for the American People": Franklin Delano Roosevelt's acceptance speech given at the Democratic National Convention in Chicago, July 2, 1932. Available here: www.presidency.ucsb.edu/ws/?pid=75174.

136 "Must the country remain hungry . . . bold, persistent experimentation": Smith, location 5797.

136 "unspoken dignity, an impenetrable reserve that protected him against undue familiarity": Smith, location 5198.

137 "disliked being disagreeable . . . particular interest was": Eleanor Roosevelt, *Autobiography*, 129.

138 "If the infantile paralysis didn't kill him, the Presidency won't": Smith, location 5676.

9. Action, and Action Now

139 "The presidency is preeminently a place of moral leadership": Burns, location 3008.

141 "enemies" and "purity": Paxton, 137.

142–143 Karen Stenner and Jonathan Haidt: "Authoritarianism is not a momentary madness," contained in Sunstein's collection of essays, *Authoritarianism: Can it Happen Here?*, 142–143.

146 "cooperative commonwealth": Brinkley, 26.

147 "Too many people are starving to death!": Burns, location 2931.

148 "This is a day . . . Action, and action now": Burns, location 3170.

150 "I just want to talk for a few minutes . . . agriculture turning around": *Fireside Chats*, 2–5.

150 "it is safer to keep your money in a reopened bank than it is to keep it under your mattress": *Fireside Chats*, 2–5.

152 "the best newspaperman who has ever been President of the United States": Goodwin, p. 26.

152 "plain, ordinary Mrs. Roosevelt" Lash, 444.

153 "It's probably . . . This is where government comes in": *Fireside Chats*, 9.

157 "a national debt, if it is not excessive, will be to us a national blessing": Hamilton to Robert Morris, April 30 1781, available here: founders.archives.gov/documents/Hamilton/01-02-02-1167

159 "During all the time I was gone . . . you don't need to tell me anything else": Leuchtenburg, 2.

159 "In broad terms I assert . . . a matter of social duty": Smith, location 5545.

159 "those who seek special political privilege and second, those who seek special financial privilege": *Fireside Chats*, 23.

160 "Are you better off today . . . Is your bank account more secure?": *Fireside Chats*, 23.

160 One scholar argued that there was, in fact, an underlying principal guiding Roosevelt's New Deal: Roosevelt's core conviction that those in need are not free: Rauschway, 4.

10. A Switch in Time Saves Nine

161 "Some people can never understand . . . until the right time comes": Alsop, 112.

162 "You know my Missus gets around a lot . . . My Missus says": Goodwin, 81.

162 "She saw many things . . . because she had a poignant understanding": Perkins said people often gave the president credit for his intuitive understanding of laborers, but his intuition came from "his recollections of what she had told him.": Goodwin, 28.

162 "unique partnership that would help change the face of the country": Goodwin, 39.

162 "They were a team . . . consequence of the partnership": Lash, xv.

163 "Missy was the real wife . . . in a nineteenth-century novel": Goodwin, 274.

165 "After considerable practice . . . handle a revolver if I had to have one in my possession": Eleanor Roosevelt, *Autobiography*, 176.

168 "to all a feeling of security as they look toward old age": *Fireside Chats*, 34.

168 "I am going to get social security . . . I will get along very well":
Eleanor, *Autobiography*, 180.

169 "I tell them it is neither fish nor fowl, but whatever it is will taste
awfully good to the People of the Tennessee Valley" Jenkins:
Roosevelt: The American Presidents, 1010.

169 "invades the reserved power of the States": *United States v. Butler*,
297 U.S. 1 (1936)

173 "eyes, ears, and legs": Burns, location 9260.

174 "I can always say, 'well, that's my wife: I can't do anything about
her'": Goodwin, 164.

174 "Convinced by the fair play . . . America's truly liberal party, the
Democrats": Easterling, "Voters Swing to New Deal."

175 "Franklin is on his own now": Lash, 567.

175 "For one reason or another . . . filled the void": Eleanor Roosevelt,
Autobiography, 185.

175 "There is one issue . . . people must be either for me or against me":
Smith, location 7914.

176 "economic royalists" and "the old enemies of peace . . . monopoly,
speculation, reckless banking": Brinkley, 54.

176 "They are unanimous in their hatred for me . . . these forces met
their master": Brinkley, 54.

177 "For twelve . . . which is the most indifferent": Burns, 5329.

178 "younger" justices who have "personal experience and contact with
modern facts and circumstances": *Fireside Chats*, 48.

11. The Second World War

180 "This generation of Americans has a rendezvous with destiny":
From Roosevelt's Re-Nomination Acceptance Speech, 1936.

181 "The news of the past few days . . . twentieth-century civilization":
Online Manuscript Collection, FDR library, www.fdrlibrary.marist
.edu/_resources/images/sign/fdr_22.pdf.

185 "Of course not . . . They're coming to see my house":
Goodwin, 73.

185 "It has come at last . . . God help us all": Smith, location 9482.

185 "I shall at all times welcome it if you would keep in touch with
me personally with everything you want me to know about":
Goodwin, 33.

186 "Until four-thirty this morning . . . invasion of Poland by Germany":
Fireside Chats, 75.

186 "maintain as a national policy . . . to a crippled humanity": *Fireside
Chats*, 75.

187 "I do not want to run again unless between now and the convention
things get much worse in Europe": Jenkins, location 1420.

188 American armed forces was ranked sixteenth in the world, trailing
Germany, Japan, France, England, Belgium, and Romania: Different
historians give slightly different rankings.

189 "defense hysteria": Goodwin, 47.

189 "meddling with affairs abroad": Goodwin, 47.

189 "If I should die tomorrow . . . Lindbergh is a Nazi": Goodwin, 48.

191 "had no wish to be a . . . free to vote for any candidate": Goodwin
(this entire incident through to "We Want Roosevelt") 124–125.

196 "At last we have gotten together . . . I like him . . . large and small":
Smith, 10905.

12. Back to the Hudson

199 "The only limit to our realization of tomorrow will be our thoughts
of today": From an undelivered address prepared for Jefferson Day,
April 13, 1945. Available here: clintonwhitehouse2.archives.gov/
WH/New/html/fdr-remarks.html

200 "California was given by God . . . keep it as he gave it to us": Smith,
location 12008.

200 "We might as well be honest": Smith, location 12001.

201 "Those Americans who believed . . . imitate the tactics of the ostrich": *Fireside Chats,* 96.

201–202 "warn the Nazis . . . be of service to your people in this tragic moment": Smith, 13273.

203 "There were toasts and more toasts . . . speech followed another": Goodwin, 476.

203 "we would lose the war": Goodwin, 476.

203 "We have differing customs . . . ourselves and the world": Goodwin, 477.

206–207 "I believe the nation is morally obligated to provide this training and education and the necessary financial assistance [to its veterans]": Smith, location 12739.

207 "All that is within me . . . our chosen form of government are at stake": Goodwin, 524.

210 "I only wish . . . she didn't have so many other engagements": Goodwin, 567–568.

210 "I hope this will come to pass": Goodwin, 568.

14. Legacy

217 "than any power since the Roman Empire. And it had a central government commensurate with that role": Leuchenburg, 5.

Bibliography

Online Resources

Franklin D. Roosevelt Presidential Library and Museum website: fdrlibrary.org, including the timeline here: www.fdrlibrary.marist. edu/archives/resources/timeline.html.

United States Constitution, full text available here: www.law.cornell.edu/ constitution/overview.

United States Senate website: www.senate.gov

Books

Alsop, Joseph. FDR: *A Centenary Remembrance*. New York, NY: Viking Press, 1982.

Brinkley, Alan. *Franklin Delano Roosevelt*. New York, NY: Oxford University Press, 2010.

Burns, James MacGregor. *Roosevelt: The Lion and the Fox (1882–1940)*. Kindle Edition. New York: Open Road Media, 2012.

Cook, Blanche Wiesen. *Eleanor Roosevelt: Vol. 1, 1884–1933, The Early Years*. New York, NY: Penguin Books, 1992.

———. *Eleanor Roosevelt: Vol. 2, 1933–1938, The Defining Years*. New York, NY: Penguin Books, 1999.

Goodwin, Doris Kearns. *No Ordinary Time: Franklin and Eleanor Roosevelt: The Home Front in World War II*. New York, NY: Simon & Schuster, 1994.

Gould, Lewis L. *Bull Moose on the Stump: The 1912 Campaign Speeches of Theodore Roosevelt*. Lawrence, KS: University Press of Kansas, 2008.

———. *Grand Old Party: A History of the Republicans*. New York, NY: Random House, 2003.

Leighton, Isabel and Gabrielle Forbrush. *My Boy Franklin: As Told by Mrs. James Roosevelt*. New York, NY: R. Long & R. R. Smith, 1933.

Paxton, Robert O. *The Anatomy of Fascism*. New York, NY: Random House, 2004.

Rauchway, Eric. *The Great Depression and the New Deal: A Very Short Introduction*. New York, NY: Oxford University Press, 2008.

Roosevelt, Eleanor. *The Autobiography of Eleanor Roosevelt*. New York, NY: HarperCollins, 1961.

Roosevelt, Franklin D. *The Fireside Chats of Franklin Delano Roosevelt*. Rockville, MD: Arc Manor, 2009.

———. *F.D.R.: His Personal Letters—Early Years*. New York, NY: Duell, Sloan and Pearce, 1947. See archive.org/stream/in.ernet .dli.2015.129582/2015.129582.Fdr-His-Personal-Letters-1928-1945_ djvu.txt.

Smith, Jean Edward. *FDR*. New York, NY: HarperCollins, 2007.

Ward, Geoffrey C. *A First-Class Temperament: The Emergence of Franklin Roosevelt, 1905–1928*. New York, NY: Vintage Books, 1989.

———. *Before the Trumpet: Young Franklin Roosevelt, 1882–1905*. New York, NY: Vintage Books, 1985. Kindle Edition.

Articles

Easterling, Louis. "Voters Swing to New Deal: A Political Revolution," *The Baltimore Afro-American*, September 12, 1936.

King, Gilbert. "The History of the Teddy Bear: From Wet and Angry to Soft and Cuddly," Smithsonian.com. See www.smithsonianmag. com/history/the-history-of-the-teddy-bear-from-wet-and-angry-to-soft-and-cuddly-170275899.

Saunders, Benjamin A., and Josephine Ngo. "The Right-Wing Authoritarianism Scale." Available here: www.researchgate.net/ publication/318260321_The_Right-Wing_Authoritarianism_Scale.

Stenner, Karen, and Jonathan Haidt. "Authoritarianism is not a Momentary Madness But an Eternal Dynamic Within Liberal Democracies," in *Can It Happen Here: Authoritarianism in America,* ed. by Cass Sunstein, published by Dey Street Books, New York, NY; 2018.

Supreme Court Case

A. L. A. *Schechter Poultry Corporation v. United States*, 295 U.S. 495 (1935)
United States v. Butler, 297 U.S. (1936)

Acknowledgments

S pecial thanks to the reference librarians at the Franklin Delano Roosevelt Library for their help in tracking down images and sources. And thank you once more to the dedicated and talented team at Abrams: Howard Reeves, a creative and insightful editor; Emily Daluga and Sara Sproull, who hold all the pieces together; designers Sara Corbett and Siobhán Gallagher, who turn mere manuscripts into works of art; managing editor Amy Vreeland, who does a lot of the heavy lifting; marketing team members Nicole Schaefer and Mary Marolla; and copyeditor Tom McNellis and proofreader Regina Castillo.

Special thank you to the Carole Greeley, who reads my manuscripts and saves me from countless embarrassing errors, and of course, Andy Schloss.

Index

Note: Page numbers in *italics* refer to illustrations.